ADVANCE PRAISE

"In a coming-of-age account set in an era of despicable segregation, Annie Waxman movingly relates her rebellion against her abusive father who, along with her mother, despised her decision to love James, a young African American man. Waxman supplies a balanced, complex portrait of James, who, albeit likable and attractive, is burdened with deeply con-flicted attitudes toward women, Whites, and himself. Equally laudable is her deeply self-reflective, insightful account of her resistance to racism and her struggle to survive severe codependency. Annie's vivacious personality animates every page of this terrific autobiography."

—DR. KEITH MILLER
Emeritus Professor of English, Arizona State University,
author of *Martin Luther King's Biblical Epic: His Great, Final Speech*

"Once I started reading *Accidental Rebel*, I couldn't stop. I felt the young naive efforts of Annie to forge her own way despite the racism of the 1960s and 70s. Luckily, when I began dating my Black, now former husband, in the early 1980s in Michigan, I didn't face the violence, secrecy, and estrangement from my parents that Annie did. Her memoir demonstrates the honesty and grit of a life lived with naiveté and the stubborn willingness to prove that love is love."

—RENEE PARKS
author of *Finally Joy: An Inspiring Guide from Collecting Joy to Creating Joy*,
mother and grandmother to nine multiracial children

"Annie Waxman's *Accidental Rebel* is one of the most powerful, moving books I've read in years. As a Black woman married to a White man, reading Annie's story gave me profound insights into the emotional and societal complexities interracial couples faced in the Jim Crow era. Her refreshing perspective doesn't gloss over the advantages of White privilege but squarely confronts it. At the core of Annie's story is the unyielding power of love. My grandchildren, who mended bonds that once seemed irreparable, symbolize the future Annie's story envisions."

—DR. CARI SKRDLA
Founder and CEO of LifeBack, LLC,
and Lady Boss Alliance, LLC

Accidental REBEL

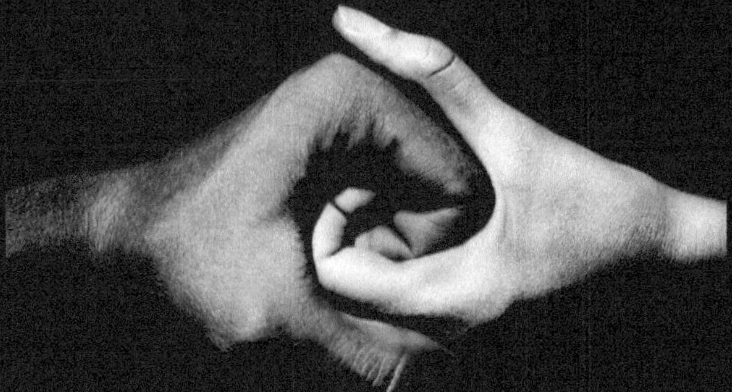

Accidental
REBEL

My Story of Interracial
LOVE AND LOSS

Annie Waxman

Editors
Laura L. Bush, PhD, peacockproud.com
Charles Grosel, write4success.net

Cover and Interior Design
Medlar Publishing Solutions Pvt Ltd., India

DISCLAIMER:
This is a work of nonfiction. The information is of a general nature to help readers know and understand more about interracial dating, interracial marriage, and civil rights. Readers of this publication agree that Annie Waxman and Peacock Proud Press will not be held responsible or liable for damages that may be alleged or resulting directly or indirectly from their use of this publication. All external links are provided as a resource only and are not guaranteed to remain active for any length of time. The author or publisher cannot be held accountable for the information provided by, or actions resulting from, accessing these resources.

DISCLAIMER

In the interest of fair play and privacy, I've changed or obscured most of the places and character names in this book, including my own.

DEDICATION

Honestly, I wrote this book for myself.
It's been a cathartic healing experience.

Now that it's finished,
I dedicate it to you, the reader.

If you experience even a glimpse of deeper understanding,
forgiveness, and love, it will have been worth the effort.

TABLE OF CONTENTS

FOREWORD

As someone who has experienced anti-interracial couple hate during my teens and my adulthood, I was both triggered and comforted by Annie Waxman's life story. At the expense of her and James's own innocence—and their physical and behavioral health as an interracial couple in the 1960s—their experience helped make my experience, and those of millions of other interracial couples living decades after them, less bleak and brutal.

Annie's rebelliousness may have been "accidental," but using her narrative to help herself heal, educates and reminds us during these hostile times, of the dark consequences of dehumanization and the brilliant power of unconditional love. As a human being and a professional historian, I am grateful for Annie's willingness and ability to chronicle and undress America's hateful underbelly, which was upheld by those who "loved" her. I am also inspired by her strength, resilience, and capacity for forgiveness in the face of her own loss and trauma.

By sharing her account and exposing this little-known history of race and interracial relationships in America, Annie shows how she was one of the courageous White kids who risked their lives and dared to love across the color line. Young people like her sacrificed their power and privilege at the altar of goodness and reason. Reading Annie's story will give the White millennial, Z, and alpha generations a relatable example of what true allyship requires: courage, selflessness, sacrifice, a sense of adventure, and bit of naive, reckless abandon.

Accidental Rebel: My Story of Interracial Love and Loss is a powerful testament and a much-needed addition to U.S history, as well as the history of race and racism in our ongoing experiment in interracial democracy. This story will resonate with many people, and as the number of interracial couples continues to grow, they should know more about the everyday people who made their relationships possible.

—Dr. Matthew Whitaker
Author of *Race Work: The Rise of Civil Rights in the Urban West* and Founder and CEO of Diamond Strategies, LLC

INTRODUCTION

I was born in the fifties. June 1952. Annie Waxman, born to Angelica and Woodrow Waxman. My older sister Mary had been born two years earlier. Claire, our younger sister, arrived eight years later.

My birthday put me smack in the middle of the tidal waves of social change that roared through the 1960s,[1] the first half as a pre-teen, the second as a popular teenage cheerleader from a well-to-do family in a small town in Kentucky, population about 9,000 the year I was born.[2]

In society at large, much was changing, with protests against the Vietnam War, political movements promoting women's and minorities' rights, cultural revolutions in literature, music, and film, and

---

[1] "The Sixties: Moments in Time," PBS, accessed September 19, 2024, https://www.pbs.org/opb/thesixties/timeline/timeline_text.html.

[2] "1950 Census of Population Preliminary Counts, Population of Kentucky by Counties, April 1, 1950," U.S. Department of Commerce, Bureau of the Census, September 5, 1950, https://www2.census.gov/library/publications/decennial/1950/pc-02/pc-2-31.pdf.

greater sexual openness with the advent of the Pill, Free Love, and Gay Liberation. In the summer of 1963, Dr. Martin Luther King Jr. gave his "I Have a Dream" speech in front of the Lincoln Memorial. Almost one year later, the Civil Rights Act of 1964 ended segregation in public places and banned employment discrimination on the basis of race, color, religion, sex, or national origin. As a result of his inspiration and leadership, Dr. King was awarded the 1964 Nobel Peace Prize. In 1967, in *Loving v. Virginia*, the Supreme Court unanimously ruled that state laws banning interracial marriage were unconstitutional. With that decision, the court made such laws illegal in the sixteen states that still had them on the books, including my home state of Kentucky.

But people don't really like change. Change threatens their worldview. Dr. King was assassinated in April 1968. Two months later, Robert Kennedy, the liberal Democrat vying for the presidential nomination, was shot down and killed at a campaign event. Five months later, Richard Nixon was elected president on a "law and order" ticket that promised a return to "the good old days"—code then, as it is now, for a return to a world order in which White men are in charge, and everyone else knows their place. Since then, the battle for change has been fought state by state, county by county, town by town. Some places resisted change more than others. Our town was one of them.

Like many small towns, ours was dragged into the sixties kicking and screaming. In my high school (class of 1970), the girls still wore skirts or dresses to school—no slacks or, God forbid, blue jeans—and the boys wore dress trousers and collared shirts with loops on the back to hang them in their lockers for gym class or after-school sports.

And though our high school had been integrated since it opened in 1963, our town schools, as a whole, had been integrated since only 1956. My sister Mary's first-grade class was one of the first integrated classes, with its two Black students.

In fact, you could say that our high school was integrated in name only. Black students were such a small minority, they were virtually invisible. Black and White students kept to themselves, clustering in their own groups in the classrooms and cafeteria, and ignoring each other in the hallway bustle, managing at most a perfunctory "Hi" if they knew each other from classes or other activities. The main venues where Black and White people spent time together were on the sports teams: basketball, football, baseball, and track and field. We had a golf team too, but since most of the golfers came from the country club, and Black people were not allowed to join the country club, there were no Black athletes on the golf team. There were no Black girls on the cheerleading squad either, even though Black athletes made up a good share of the teams the cheerleaders cheered for.

Sports were for boys. Girls didn't have athletic teams unless you counted the cheerleading squad, which I most certainly did. The truth about cheerleading is that it is a demanding physical sport, a combination of dance and gymnastics. It requires athleticism, strength, endurance, and agility. You couldn't last half a practice if you weren't in good shape. I know. I had been a cheerleader since elementary school and for the first three years of high school. Cheerleading was at the center of my school life, the core of my high school identity. I enjoyed the physical aspects of performing, but also, I have to admit, I loved the attention.

Black and White students didn't mingle much outside of school either. Black students stayed in "their" part of town, which had an offensive name, Bucktown, I'm ashamed to say. At the same time, the thriving Black business district supported Black-owned businesses, including grocery stores, retail stores, commercial properties, professional firms, restaurants, bars, and pool halls. Generally, Black folks only crossed into the White parts of town for work, usually some form of domestic or manual labor. When I was young, my family owned a tobacco farm, and most of the farmhands were Black. Black maids also helped Mom iron and vacuum and scrub the floors, as they did in most of the homes of the well-to-do.

I remember two farmhands in particular: Jim and another whom we called "Georgie Porge." It's embarrassing that I don't remember his formal name. At the time, White people calling Black people belittling nicknames was common. I used to eat lunch with "the help," as my mother called them, on the porch where she served them. I was fascinated by Georgie's coarse hair and ran my hands through it whenever I had the chance. It upsets me to think of that now, the arrogance and intrusiveness, the violation of boundaries. He said he didn't mind, but how could he say no to the boss's young daughter?

Our family ventured into the Black part of town for only one reason. My mother bought cherry furniture from a Black woodworker, the finest woodworker in the county. When I was about eight, Mom and I drove to his shop so Mom could explain what she wanted next and to pick up the finished pieces that fit in the car. It was always fascinating to see the different parts of town, the smaller yards, the tiny houses squeezed in next to each other, the Black children playing in the yards and the streets. Not that we spent much time there. We drove straight to the shop, then straight home, so what I saw was through the car window. Even so, it felt odd to be some of the few White people driving the streets, as though we were the outsiders, which we were, of course. I wasn't afraid exactly. It was more like I was hyperaware of how different I was from the people who lived there. Looking back, I think this gave me a small (a very, very small) sense of what people of color might feel much of their lives in majority White spaces.

It was an odd and confusing time. We were taught to respect the maids and farmhands and were scolded at family dinners if we said anything remotely disparaging, let alone racist. At the same time, there were unwritten rules about the races we understood and followed. Black people were the mysterious and "exotic other." We were to be friendly with our Black classmates and the Black townspeople we met, but not friends. And under no circumstances should the two races even *think* about dating across those lines. That was still a very strict taboo when I was growing up.

Other archaic Jim Crow customs prevailed. We attended and participated in minstrel shows—musical revues with songs and dances performed by White people in blackface, a fact of which I am ashamed of now. At the time, though, we thought nothing of it. It's what you did if you were White and lived in Kentucky, as well as many other states across the country, and not just in the South.

The town had only one movie house when I was growing up. It opened in 1925 and hadn't changed much since then, with its plaster scrollwork of cherubs and theatrical masks on the walls and ceiling and the heavy dark curtains that parted once the main feature lit up the single screen. Outside, the marquee was secured to the building by a rusty metal frame. In the shadow of the marquee, the ticket booth split the entranceway like an island in a stream.

Until I was in the eighth grade, as I remember it, the theater had separate entrances for Black and White people, and the seating was segregated as well. White people went through the large doors on either side of the ticket booth. These led to the main floor. Black people went through smaller doors outside the theater. These led to narrow stairways that took them up to the balcony. My friends and I would get there early to grab the seats under the balcony to avoid the shower of popcorn, candy wrappers, and empty cups and cartons that rained from above. If one of those friends happened to be a boy I liked, then the seats under the balcony were ideal for making out as well.

There were other signs that change was coming only slowly to our town. My sister Mary tells the story of a high school basketball game in 1968. The majority of the starters that year were Black. At the beginning of the first game, when they noticed the composition of the starting team, two of the most popular White guys in Mary's class stood up and walked out.

"Where are you going?" Mary challenged them. "Why are you leaving?"

"We're not going to watch a bunch of n*****s play for our team," one of them responded for both.

Mary was astonished at their blatant racism. She made a point to stay for the whole game and cheer loudly.

My friend Bobby was the only White starter on that team. I had known Bobby since elementary school, and because I was a cheerleader and he played basketball, we became closer friends in junior high and high school. Not only was he a very good point guard, but he was a very good student and one of the nicest guys and best friends you'd ever want to meet. He was always there when I needed him.

Bobby experienced our town's ingrained racism firsthand that season. White people he didn't even know got in his face and said things like, "What kind of family lets their son play with a bunch of n*****s?" Taunts like these opened Bobby's eyes to issues of social justice, which he has been addressing as an educator ever since.

Despite incidents like these, my family, friends, and I were too often oblivious to racism, both hidden and overt. We lived in our own world of privilege, and we naively believed that just about everyone in our town was treated fairly and equally—as long as they stayed in line and followed the unspoken rules.

The assassination of Dr. Martin Luther King Jr. opened some of our eyes to the plight of Black people in our town and the rest of the United States. Bobby tells of the day after Dr. King was killed. He was changing classes and overheard a White guy in the hall say, "I'm glad they killed the n*****." Marvin, a Black football player, heard what the White student said and went after him, beating him fairly badly. Most people in the hall cheered Marvin on, White people included. Some attitudes *were* changing, if slowly.

My friend Henry, who is Black, talks about his own experiences with racism in the South. He grew up in a three-room house in the Mississippi Delta with nine brothers and sisters. Not three bedrooms, he emphasizes—three *rooms*. His family was very poor. In the South, Henry felt lost, he explains, invisible, especially in the 1960s. As a Black man, if a White man said something to you, no matter how absurd or offensive, you couldn't say anything back. You had to walk a very fine line. And if you looked at a White woman too long or in what White people interpreted as the *wrong way*, a group of White men would come to your house at night and teach you a lesson. It was an old world, Henry observes. If you were Black, it was safer to stay in your part of town. That way you didn't have to worry about crossing a line you might not even know existed. You dealt with your own people. This was safer and more practical, but it also held Black people back, socially and economically. Henry never felt comfortable in his own skin until he followed one of his brothers to Los Angeles to attend college. Los Angeles has long been known for its acceptance of a broad mix of cultures. This is where I became friends with Henry and his wife Mary, who was from Trinidad and of Indo-European descent.

Along with Missouri, Maryland, and Delaware, Kentucky was one of four slave states that joined the Confederacy during the Civil War. And Kentucky as a state did not ratify the Thirteenth Amendment abolishing slavery until 1976. I was twenty-four years old.

Our town reflects that history. When I was growing up, the town had all the attributes of a small southern town, old-fashioned in its beliefs about race relations, including the nonsense about "separate but equal" and Black people "knowing their place."

I'm not saying this to excuse the town's worldview and behavior. That is certainly not what I believed then, let alone believe now. But I really wasn't an activist, and I didn't think about these kinds of societal issues at any great depth growing up. I was a very social teenager who liked to have fun, a mostly good girl who tried to please her parents and got into no more than the usual amount of teenage trouble.

I never set out to be a rebel, to shatter the social norms of the time, but despite myself, that's what I became: an accidental rebel. And I did so by doing what sixteen-year-olds the world over have done time immemorial.

I fell in love.

But the guy I fell in love with—James—was Black in a time and place where such a relationship was still taboo to the point of revulsion for way too many of our fellow townspeople—including my own parents. That was our mortal sin, according to the town we both lived in, our shame, that we dared to date "across the color line," as many in the town would have put it. What happened to me and James changed our lives forever. I'm still dealing with the fallout more than fifty years later, though James and I are no longer together. I have more than fifteen years of therapy under my belt, and I'm not finished yet.

I shouldn't—and won't—speak for James. He's a private man who has his own demons and keeps his own counsel, and I doubt he'll ever tell his side of the story. I'm not speaking for my sisters either, who are still alive, or my parents, who are not. This is my part of the story, the story I need to tell to understand the trauma of what happened to me when I dared to date a Black man in a small town in Kentucky in the late 1960s and how it shaped me into who I am today.

One final note before I go on. If I'm going to tell my story with any degree of accuracy, I have to reveal unpleasant truths—about the town I grew up in, about my family, and even about me. I don't intend to offend anyone, but I'm not going to let anyone off the hook either, least of all myself. With the benefit of hindsight, I realize now that when I was with James, I sometimes thought and acted in ways that were influenced by the racism I was brought up with, that just because I dated and married a Black man didn't mean I was automatically freed from my position of privilege and biases as a White woman born into a wealthy family. Many of my decisions were informed by that privilege. I wasn't always aware enough to consider James's perspective as a Black man. Our state had legalized interracial marriages just two years before we started dating. I didn't know about that law then, and even if I had, I'm not sure I would have understood the implications—that, of the two of us, James was in *much* greater danger of violence than I was. (Although I experienced my own trauma as the result of our relationship.)

It was an ugly time in the country in many ways, but things were changing. Unfortunately, they didn't change fast enough to keep me from getting caught between the rock and the hard place of racism and misogyny.

Chapter 1

MY MOM AND DADDY

To understand my story, you need to know about my parents. Daddy was a World War II pilot in the United States Army Air Forces, and Mom was the Polish German war bride he fell in love with and defied his parents to bring to the United States.

My parents met in a dental office in West Germany that served American soldiers, where Mom worked as a hygienist after the war. For Mom to enter the United States, my father's parents (my paternal grandparents, William and Betty Waxman) had to sign certain papers, as family lore has it, but they refused. They were country folk, tobacco farmers in Kentucky. The Germans had been our enemy in the war. They didn't want any "Nazis" in the family!

Daddy was a stubborn one, though, and deeply in love. He told his parents he'd never speak to them again if they didn't sign the papers, that this was the woman he loved, that he was going to marry her, and that was that. Daddy can be very persuasive when he wants to be, and eventually his parents gave in, and here we all are.

(My father and I were a lot alike, when you think about it. I did something similar with James more than twenty years later.)

The United States had strict immigration quotas in those days, but the War Brides Acts of 1945 and 1946 stipulated that war brides and other dependents of US citizens wouldn't be counted against these quotas.[3] These acts also provided the war brides free transportation to the United States. That's how Mom ended up flying to the States in 1947 on a plane filled with other European war brides on their way to reunite with their husbands or fiancés. They flew into New York, then Mom caught another flight to meet Daddy in Houston, where he had been stationed on his return from Europe. That's where they were married in a small wedding at the courthouse, with Daddy's war buddy Butch the best man and a friend of Mom's from Hungary the maid of honor.

Once Daddy left the service, the newlyweds moved back home, where my father bought his own tobacco farm on the opposite side of town from his parents' farm and the farms of his brother, Uncle George, and his sisters, Aunt Clara and Aunt Dorothy. Mary and I lived on the farm with Mom and Daddy until about 1960, when our younger sister Claire was born. I remember the seemingly endless neat rows of tobacco plants at different heights depending on the season. There was also a good-sized curing barn, where the harvested leaves were hung upside down from floor to ceiling until they turned brown and could be baled and sold.

This move to a Kentucky farm must have been quite a shock for Mom, who had been born in the village of Tröbsdorf in 1924 and lived as a girl and young woman with her Catholic family in another small village in Germany. Not only did Mom have to learn

---

[3] "Coming to America: The War Brides Act of 1945," The National WWII Museum, New Orleans, December 18, 2020, https://www.nationalww2museum.org/war/articles/war-brides-act-1945.

a new language and a new way of life in the United States, but she had to put up with the rural prejudices against foreigners. That may explain why she always tried to keep us in line, always tried to make sure we were well-mannered and well-behaved. She may have felt that as an immigrant in a small town, she already had a target on her back. She didn't want to draw any more attention to herself or the rest of the family.

She was a tough one, though, and it helped that she wasn't the only new German bride in the county. She and Dad met Helga and John, who had three boys and lived up the street. Our two families became friendly, sharing meals and cookouts, attending dances, playing cards. Mom and Helga got together most afternoons to sneak a cigarette and chat in German so we couldn't understand what they were saying. They tried to hide what they were doing, but we could smell the cigarette smoke drifting from under the bedroom door.

Mom loved to dance. She was a great beauty, with a nice figure, and wore high heels her whole life to show off her dancer's legs. Mom wasn't always open with us at home—she was somewhat stern, in fact—but she came alive on the dance floor. Watching how happy she was when she danced always made me feel happier as well.

My friend Grace, whom I have known since we were four years old, remembers that Mom wore nothing but heels, even when she was cooking or doing housework. (Grace was not only a childhood friend, but she has also been a friend all my life. We still get together at least twice a year to catch up and renew our friendship. We met as children, but we became best friends in junior high and high school. She was also a cheerleader and an important witness to my story.)

Besides, adjusting to a new life in the United States was nothing compared to what Mom had gone through during the war. I found out recently that before Mom met Daddy, she had been engaged to a German soldier who had been killed in battle. She had never talked about her German fiancé and how devastating that must have been to lose him.

There were two stories Mom did tell—and more than once. The first took place in the middle of the war. One day Mom was riding her bicycle in the village where she lived with her family, doing errands, trying to scavenge what she could of the scarce supplies left to the villagers. She heard a train running on the little-used tracks on the village outskirts; then she heard another sound she couldn't make out at first, an unnerving keening that gave her the shivers. She listened closely, then figured it out. It was the people on the train, wailing and weeping, a chorus of agony that wouldn't let up.

When she got home, she asked her mother who was on that train. Her mother told her she didn't really know, but she'd heard rumors that many of the mainline tracks had been bombed out, and some of the trains filled with Jews had been rerouted past their village. No one really knew where the Jews were being taken because the camps weren't talked about openly, but they assumed it was nowhere good.

This upset Mom in a profound way. Some of their village friends were Jewish and made to wear yellow stars. It was personal for her. She worried for her friends and prayed for those on the trains.

The other story she told us was how she ended up in the dental office in West Germany, attending to the teeth of American soldiers.

Near the end of the war, everything was in chaos. The Western Allies—the United States, Great Britain, and France—were invading from the west, and the Russians (technically the Soviets) from the east. The four groups had already divided Germany into four sectors, and it was known that the Soviet sector would remain in the USSR's sphere of influence after the war. (This area would become the German Democratic Republic, commonly known as East Germany.) The village where Mom still lived with her family was on the western edge of the Soviet sector. You could see into the American sector from the village!

Mom's family were German citizens but of Polish Catholic descent. There was no love lost between the Poles and the Russians, and many Polish families were fleeing to the safety of the West. My mother was the youngest of six sisters, two of whom had died by then. Two of the remaining sisters, Aunt Lucia and Aunt Pia, had already made their escape to the West. Mom wanted to join them, but she was torn. Her parents wouldn't leave, and neither would her other sister, Aunt Johanna. This was their home, they explained. Why should they leave? One government was much like the next.

Meanwhile, Soviet artillery shells were drawing closer, and it would only be a matter of days before the troops followed. Mom had to decide. She knew that once the Russians "liberated" the village, they would close the border, and it would be too late to leave. The shelling intensified, leveling many of the village's buildings. It became more and more dangerous to stay. One day my mother and a friend looked at each other, afraid of what was coming, and without a word, they hopped on their bikes and rode toward the American sector with the shells exploding in the village behind them.

Her friend got cold feet at the border and turned back, but Mom kept going, successfully crossing to the American side. Many of the details are fuzzy. In what became West Germany, Mom eventually found a room in a boarding house for young women. While there, she trained as a dental hygienist and got a job in West Berlin, where she met my father.

Mom never saw her parents again, though they kept in touch by letter and the rare international phone call. I never met my maternal grandparents. They were stuck behind the Iron Curtain and died there. Mom tried to see them before the end of their lives, but this was before the Berlin Wall had come down. The US government couldn't guarantee Mom's safety while she was in East Germany, nor could they guarantee she would be able to return once she crossed the border. The East German government still thought of people like her as citizens of East Germany. She had her home and family in the United States, and she couldn't take the risk. It broke her heart. She kept her feelings to herself, but every time her parents came up in conversation, a sad, distant look darkened her face, and she quickly changed the subject.

That's about all she would tell us about the war. When most other topics came up, she slammed shut like a bank vault, locking her secrets deep inside her heart, but she'd have nightmares for weeks afterward. Toward the end of her life, she told us that she had a dark secret from the war she couldn't tell anyone. *What is it?* the three of us daughters would ask at different times in different ways, hoping she'd give in and tell us. But she never did. Just as she vowed, she took that secret to the grave, and to this day we can only guess what it might have been. That was Mom. When she set out to do something, she did it, and she could never be persuaded otherwise. I inherited that trait from her.

Mom did not have an easy life, and it wasn't easy for her to open up or show affection. I never held that against her. She spoke with her actions, and though Daddy wouldn't allow us to be baptized in the Catholic Church—we always went to Methodist services—she raised us in the Catholic way, loving but strict, and taught us to be respectful and kind, follow the rules, and say "Please" and "Thank you." She was a good mom, practically a single mother, since Daddy wasn't around much after we moved from the farm. I loved her until the day she died, and she loved me, though the story I'm about to tell put that love to a grave test.

Daddy loved me too, but where Mom was stern and conducted herself with stoic German discipline, Daddy was outgoing and energetic, a natural-born salesman. But he had periods of deep depression and a mean streak that came out when he was drinking—and he drank all the time. He was an alcoholic. Recently, I learned that clinical depression runs in his family, which explains why he was treated eight times with electroshock therapy when I was in college. He may also have suffered PTSD from the war, but he never talked about it and never sought help. He used alcohol as a form of self-medication.

Daddy being Daddy, he had a much different war than Mom. For one thing, he was a cocky American on the winning side. For another, with his entrepreneurial personality, he thrived in the Wild West atmosphere of Europe at the end of the war. He flew DC-3s on rescue-and-supply missions and told us how he held back a portion of the supplies he was supposed to deliver—cigarettes, chocolates, pantyhose, and the like—and sold them out of the back of the plane on the black market. Everyone was doing it, he explained. But even if it wasn't true that "Everyone was doing it," Daddy certainly was, and he was proud of it. We have pictures of him out in the field with his plane, the goods laid out on a ramp.

There's a plane like Daddy's on display at the Museum of Flying at the Santa Monica Airport in Los Angeles, where I have lived for more than forty-eight years. Whenever he came to visit, we drove by the airport to see the plane, and he'd tell us the stories all over again.

Maybe selling on the black market is where he learned to work the gray areas of business. I don't have proof of this, mind you, just suspicions. Once we left the farm, Daddy's first business was as a house mover—not moving furniture but moving whole houses. It was a good business to go into just then. The highway being built through the county displaced many families, and they wanted to take their houses with them. Daddy saw a great business opportunity. In fact, once we moved from the farm, Daddy moved our own house about a mile down the road. It was a neighborhood spectacle. Everyone came out to watch the backhoe dig a trench around the foundation and the crane lift the house onto a trailer. The house was so heavy that a tire on the trailer caved into the asphalt.

From there, it was a natural step for Daddy to become a home builder and a land developer, and from what I understand, there's a lot of gray areas in those businesses—knowing the right people, influencing the local government, scaring away competitors. I know very little about the details of Daddy's businesses, how he ran them, how he kept the books, how much money he actually made, but I do know that many people were afraid of him. He always boasted that he had graduated from the school of hard knocks and had the scars to prove it. He was a good ole southern boy, the black sheep of the family, and very wild. He didn't conform. He snuck out of the house as a kid. He didn't go to church. He drank. He played jokes on people. Though he wasn't a huge man at about five feet, nine inches, he was solidly built and menacing when he drank. He could also turn on the charm when he wanted to, especially with the ladies, who loved him. And he loved them back, much to my mother's dismay. This had a lot to do with why they separated when I was in high school.

One time when we still lived on the farm, Daddy shot off a guy's toe. The man had come to the farm with a friend to confront Daddy with some cockamamie story about Daddy stealing his girlfriend and keeping her in the barn. The man came to the door and said his piece. Daddy said, "What are you talking about?"

I don't know whether Daddy was messing around with this guy's girlfriend or not, and whether they had been using the barn—with what I know now, I wouldn't have put it past him—but that night there was no one in the barn. Mom was standing with Daddy. The friend of this crazy guy got out of the car carrying a gun.

Mom screamed, and Daddy told Mary and me to run upstairs and shut the door. Drunk and wild-eyed, the man tried to push his way into the house. Mom held a frying pan to fight him off, but Daddy pushed her out of the way to protect her and grabbed the shotgun from behind the door. The guy saw the shotgun, turned, and ran. Daddy followed him out into the yard and took a shot at his legs since he didn't want to kill him. He hit a toe. The man fell to his knees. His buddy ran to him, pulled him up to his feet, and he limped the rest of the way to the car, where the two of them jumped in and sped off.

Mom and Daddy called the police, who took our side since the man had been trespassing and threatening our family. Besides, Daddy was friends with just about every cop in the county, part of his business strategy. The police found the guy in the hospital getting his toe treated and ran him in on some charge or another. That was the kind of clout Daddy had.

After the shooting, Mom decided she'd had enough of living on the farm. This was about 1960. Daddy wasn't home much, and it was only by chance he was there that day. Mom was pregnant with Claire, and she wanted to move into town where she felt we'd be safer. Daddy obliged her. For all his faults, Daddy always took care of us.

I don't have many other childhood memories of Daddy. I remember riding in a pickup truck with him while we still lived on the farm. There was a huge storm, thunder cracking and lightning flashing around us. We headed to the backfield to check on the cows. Daddy got out of the truck, and while I waited for him, I grew more and more afraid of the storm. I was so scared I started seeing things. I thought I saw a woman with long white hair run through the headlights in front of the truck. I'm sure I imagined it, but it seemed so real at the time. It spooked me. I was relieved when Daddy returned, rain dripping from his hair and jacket.

"Daddy, Daddy, I saw a woman in the headlights," I said, agitated. "She had long hair."

"Nobody's out here but us," he said. "Don't you worry. You're safe."

And when he climbed into the truck and we headed back to the house, I did feel safe.

I cherish that memory. Things like that didn't happen very often. In fact, Daddy was fairly absent from my life, at least physically. (However, I always carried a great deal of emotional baggage from his behavior toward me. I still do.) I had been taking dance lessons since I was three and cheerleading since I was in the sixth grade, and he had rarely gone to any of my performances or games. He wasn't with us much once we moved from the farm. When he was, it was often unpleasant. We were used to being in the house without him and living by Mom's rules. When he showed up, we had to switch gears and live by his rules, and since he was an alcoholic, his rules were a moving target. We walked on eggshells. We never knew what would set him off. One day it would be too much sass, another that we slammed the screen doors too loud, yet another that we hadn't cleaned our rooms. Like many fathers in the fifties and sixties, Daddy expected complete and instant obedience. He was both domineering and unpredictable because of his drinking, a confusing combination for those of us trying to please him.

Even with all that, Daddy made sure we lived comfortably, providing us with everything: food, clothes, toys, school supplies, and the house itself. He was generous with money, when he had it, though as a businessman, he sometimes had cash-flow problems. He sent us money even once we were adults, perhaps to make up for the lack of time he spent with us as children. But I'm convinced he also sent us money because he truly loved us, and this was his way of showing it, of performing his fatherly duties. Money was his "love language," as they say these days. He was very loyal to us, including Mom, even once they separated. We were his family, and he took that seriously.

One thing Daddy did every year, and I remember it fondly, was to read *Twas the Night Before Christmas* on Christmas Eve. No matter what else was happening in our lives, he came to the house the night of Christmas Eve to read to us. We'd all sit in the living room in front of the Christmas tree, Mary and I on either side of him, and Claire, once she was born, on his lap. He'd read the poem from a well-thumbed copy of the book we'd had around the house for years. He always put a lot of emotion into it, reading with an expression and passion that surprised and tickled us. It was one of the rare times I felt close to him when I was young.

"'Twas the night before Christmas . . .,'" he started in a whisper. Then his voice became more urgent as he read on. "'Away to the window I flew in a flash . . .'" And he ended with a loud flourish: "'Happy Christmas to all and to all a good night!'"

We giggled and said, "Read it again. Read it again."

"I can't do that," he said, as if telling us a grave secret. "Santa won't come if you don't go to sleep. Go on now. Get to bed."

Reluctantly, we scrambled into bed, but it was all worth it when we got up the next morning to open presents. Christmas Day was glorious. You couldn't walk for all the gifts spreading out from under the tree into the living room. After we tore through the wrappings of those presents, we drove to my grandparents' farm and spent the rest of Christmas there, opening more presents, eating enormous quantities of wonderful food, and playing with our cousins and new toys.

At the end of Christmas Day, Daddy left us and went on his way. That was fine with us. Once the holiday was over, he could be such a negative presence with his anger and demands. We were always relieved when he left.

Chapter 2

GROWING UP
IN KENTUCKY

Don't get me wrong. Our family didn't live in constant chaos. When Daddy was on his best behavior or away from the house, we lived a very simple, small-town life that was quite enjoyable. We felt comfortable, well taken care of. We girls all went to church with Mom on Sundays, and when Daddy was home, he stayed behind and watched the Dallas Cowboys.

Sports were a major form of recreation and entertainment, from the playground to high school to the University of Kentucky. And don't forget the Kentucky Derby. We also had holiday parades and street fairs. Every summer the town closed down Main Street to put on a Hula-Hoop contest. Mom drove us into town and parked on a side street. Everybody from young kids to older teenagers (those of us who were White, anyway) were in the street spinning our colorful hoops, laughing and calling out encouragement to each other, groaning when the hoop clattered to the ground. It was a kaleido-scope of color and movement and fun. Every year Mary and I tried our hand. We got pretty good but never lasted the whole time to win a prize.

I always kept busy. I took dance from the age of three to sixteen and performed in a host of recitals, as did many of my friends, and of course there was cheerleading, which occupied a good portion of my time in junior high and high school.

Helicopter parenting wasn't a thing then, so during the summers we hopped on our bikes after breakfast and sometimes didn't return until we heard our mothers ring their bells at dinnertime. Every family had its own bell, and when you heard yours, you jumped on your bike and sped home as fast as you could. During the day, we took turns grabbing lunch at each other's houses—nothing fancy, PB and J, bologna, or ham sandwiches. The mothers all took turns. We kept track of which families were going through hard times and made sure those kids always got something to eat.

On the long summer days, we played the usual kids' games: tag and freeze tag, red rover, hide-and-seek, kickball, touch football, and basketball. I recruited some girls to be cheerleaders for these games. We made up the cheers ourselves. On other days, we played school and put on silly skits. We liked to play *Wagon Train*, circling our little red wagons against attacks. The girls put our dolls in the wagons, and the boys wore their six-shooters and cowboy hats. I was the wagon master and organized the games.

We raced bicycles, climbed trees, and built forts and clubhouses from discarded lumber and cardboard. Sometimes we played at the creek, catching frogs, tadpoles, and crawdads. We went swimming at the country club (for those who were members) or at the houses of friends whose families were lucky enough to have an aboveground pool. When we were thirsty, we drank Kool-Aid, lemonade, and Ale-8-One (which we shortened to Ale-8), a regional soft drink with so much caffeine that we'd be wired all day. Everyone had Ale-8 in their refrigerators. Even today when I go back to Kentucky, Grace and I buy a cold Ale-8 and go for a drive. I have Ale-8 in my fridge here in California as I write this.

When things wound down at night after dinner, we played board games and card games inside screened-in porches: Chutes and Ladders, Monopoly, Life, Old Maid, and Crazy Eights. Or we'd just sit in the porch swing and listen to the crickets and watch the lightning bugs flashing their messages.

When Mary and I were kids, my parents took us to the drive-in movies about four miles up the road from our farm. We climbed into Daddy's huge baby-blue 1952 Cadillac and brought along a sack of homemade popcorn. We rolled down the windows partway and hung up the speaker. I usually fell asleep, but Mary, Mom, and Dad would stay up to finish the movie. This was strictly a family affair. Daddy was extremely strict (Grace will vouch for that), and he didn't allow us to go to the drive-in movies with friends, even in high school.

As we grew older, we had slumber parties on the weekends, especially at Linda's house in the country. She was also a cheerleader and in our close circle of friends. Once we could drive (or knew someone who could), we'd pile into a car together, about a half a dozen of us, and cruise around Jerry's Drive In restaurant. Every high school kid in town did the same thing. We'd wave to the kids in the other cars and, if we weren't driving, we'd hang out the windows and call out to each other, trying to carry on conversations from car to car. After we drove around a few times so everyone saw us and we saw them, we parked and ordered food, usually burgers and fries, which the servers brought out to the cars. Every once in a while, we'd go into the restaurant, usually after a game, and get a booth for the cheerleading squad.

I remember these parts of my childhood very fondly.

Other parts, not so much.

Both of my parents had seen and done things in the war they never talked about. Maybe because they knew what the world was capable of, they saw it as their duty to protect us. By "protect" I mean "imprison." At least that's how it felt to Mary and me as children and teenagers. Our parents' notion of what was acceptable for young ladies of the small-town upper middle class felt like shackles to us. Both my mother and father were very aware of the status my father's successful businesses lent the family and were vigilant about preserving it.

This was the era of the "what-would-people-think" morality, though my father seemed exempt from those judgments. There were many unspoken rules, like what to wear, how to act, and whom to hang out with. When I was nine and Mary was eleven, Mom had a seamstress make us black corduroy jumpers, which we wore over white blouses. The other townspeople, including Daddy's family, were aghast. They thought it was terrible that Mom made us wear black clothes in public. "What an odd, foreign notion," they whispered. "Black clothes are for funerals. Everyone knows that."

We were a newly prominent family, not old money, and all eyes were on us. My parents wouldn't let us do many of the things our friends did, like car dating, driving to the bigger city (only fifteen minutes away), or even watching basketball games with our friends at the junior high gym. When Mary attended these games, Daddy made her stand off to the side of the court with him and the tobacco farmers rather than sit with her friends in the stands. We could never really figure out why, and he never gave us an explanation. I managed to avoid this particular humiliation because I was a cheerleader.

Before Claire was born, if we violated Daddy's rules, especially the ones about talking back and expressing our own opinions, Daddy horsewhipped us just as his country parents had horsewhipped him when he got out of line. That sucker stung, believe me, and I always toed the line as best I could. I never wanted to make Daddy angry.

I was a good kid, as I remember it, but "spirited," as my parents, teachers, and relatives called me. This wasn't a compliment. I remember one time in first grade the teacher came into the room while I was sitting cross-legged on top of a table talking to the boys. She shooed me back to my own table with a stern look and scolded me: "Young ladies don't sit with their legs crossed on top of tables talking to boys." I didn't see why not. It was fun. But I always tried to mind the adults in my life, even if it didn't make sense.

Right around the time Claire was born, Mom made Daddy lose the horsewhip, and after that he enforced discipline by yelling and storming around the house, resorting to his hands and the belt on occasion. Today we'd say my father was controlling and abusive, but back then he was simply considered strict—spare the rod and spoil the child. But I have to say he was on the stricter end of the spectrum even for that time.

For example, we couldn't talk at the dinner table unless Daddy specifically asked us a question or gave us permission. Can you imagine two young girls sitting quietly at the dinner table (three once Claire was born)? We squirmed in our chairs, an offense in itself that earned the admonition to "Sit still, for Chrissake!" from Daddy. We tried our darndest to be quiet, but of course when you're a kid and somebody tells you not to do something, that's all you can think about doing.

Mary and I would fidget in our seats. Mom would notice, and her lip would twitch from holding back her laughter. Then we would let out a snicker. We couldn't help it, and Mom would pretend to wipe her mouth with a napkin so Dad couldn't see her smiling. Mary and I weren't as subtle as Mom, and when we couldn't hold it in any longer, we would burst out laughing. Mom couldn't help it either, and she would laugh with us. Dad would get so mad he would send us to our rooms without dinner. Mom could stay at the table, but she knew better than to cross him after that. They ate in virtual silence for the rest of the meal. All you could hear were the scrapes of the forks and knives on their plates and one-word answers to their attempts at conversation while Daddy kept huffing about disrespect in his own house.

Once we moved from the farm to the brick ranch home in town, Daddy had his businesses to run, so he wasn't around as much. My granddaddy and grandma continued to live on their farm out in the country. Uncle George, Aunt Clara, and Aunt Dorothy lived down the road from them, each on their own family farms. Granaddy and Grandma built a pool in the backyard, and we visited every weekend.

We didn't see them at our house very often, though, because Grandma and the aunts refused to enter the house. I'm not entirely sure why—maybe because Daddy was a drinker, and they were afraid of his ungodly ways. I don't know. They didn't drink themselves. All I know is that whenever they wanted to see us, they drove over to the house, pulled into the driveway, parked, and sat in the car. We went out and talked to them through the rolled-down window. Now if Granaddy was by himself, he might come in and eat dinner with us. But the women would not step one foot into the house. Strange, yes, looking back, but to us at the time, that was life with the relatives.

With Daddy gone so much, it was only us girls most of the time. Though Mom had a strict Catholic upbringing and tried to pass that on to us, she was never as stern as Daddy. She was more firm than severe, and we quickly learned how to get around her, especially if we wanted to spend time with our boyfriends.

Mary led the way, though she really wasn't a born troublemaker. In fact, she was the scholar of the family (still is) and did very well in school. But like all of us Waxman girls, she's a bit of a hard-ass and didn't see any reason she couldn't pick whom she wanted to date. For a time, that was Davey from the wrong side of the tracks.

Looking back, Davey wasn't that much different from us, but his family didn't have as much money. They weren't dirt poor, but they literally lived on the other side of the tracks, and that was a big deal. It was the blue-collar part of town. The houses were smaller, and the yards were in disarray, with abandoned cars rusting away in some of them and broken-down refrigerators and other appliances on the porches.

Mary had to sneak around to see Davey. As far as our parents were concerned, Mary spent a lot of time with her girlfriends, going to the movies, meeting up at the diner for burgers and milkshakes, playing records at their house, and going to band practice. Nothing too suspicious, and nothing that couldn't be explained away with an "Oh, we just changed our minds and did something else" if they were discovered in a different place. Mary was smart about it and quick on her feet. She never really got caught.

In the spring of my junior year (February 1969), I started seeing James, a basketball player at my school. When we began dating, I followed Mary's example and spent a lot of time with fictitious girlfriends. Well, the girlfriends were real, but the outings were not.

These subterfuges were even more important for me because James was Black, and at that time, a White girl dating a Black guy was still a big deal, virtually unheard of. Grace remembers a few other Black and White couples beginning to date at the same time, but that certainly wasn't even close to the norm. In fact, Kentucky was one of the states that still had laws on the books banning inter-racial marriage when *Loving v. Virginia* came down in 1967, only two years before I met James. In our town, interracial relationships were still the subject of juicy gossip.

Before James and I got together, I dated other boys and engaged in the usual teenage activities: hanging out in larger groups of boys and girls, playing spin the bottle at boy-girl parties, pairing up at school dances, and making out in the movie theater. It was nothing very serious and nothing very daring.

I was popular in high school. Not only was I Woody Waxman's daughter, but I was outgoing and friendly and made friends easily. I was also a talented cheerleader and photogenic, I was told.

I became a cheerleader because I loved the attention and was a good athlete, and in those days if you were an athletic girl, you went out for cheerleading. There were really no other options. I loved sports—still do—and cheerleading was my way to participate. When Daddy was home, we had sports on the TV whenever he could find it—the Dallas Cowboys, University of Kentucky Wildcats, basketball, football, baseball, you name it. We had seasons tickets for many of the teams, and I often went to games with Daddy, including the high school games before any of us were even in high school.

Cheerleading also meant social recognition. I received a lot of attention for being a cheerleader. Because I was one of the best, I was often out in front of the crowds in the gym or on the football field, and I frequently had my picture in the papers, both the local paper and the big-city paper. Perhaps as a result, I came out on top or near the top of many popularity contests in junior high and high school. This sounds like bragging, and maybe it is a little. I can't say I didn't like the attention. It fed me.

Until it went negative.

Our town had one pharmacy at the time, which was not the same as the corner drugstore with its lunch counter, and I went to the pharmacy often, either for my own purchases—candy, soda, magazines, and toiletries—or for Mom's prescriptions. Because I went there so often, I got to know the delivery guy, Lawrence, who was a cute Black guy. He wasn't in high school, but he wasn't much older than we were. He was friendly, and me being the social butterfly I am, we talked when he was between deliveries.

My sisters and I lived at one end of the house, and our parents' bedroom was at the other end of a long hallway. We had our own phone with our own number, and one day, Lawrence called. He must have gotten my number from someone else or looked it up in the phone book. I don't think I gave it to him, but I don't recall.

After he explained who he was, I said, "Oh, hi." I don't remember what else I thought about his calling, whether I thought it was weird or inappropriate, but southern hospitality means you don't make people feel bad if you don't have to, so I talked to him. It was kind of fun, nothing spectacular. I agreed he could call again if he wanted to. I talked to loads of people on the phone. It was how I spent much of my time at home, so it wasn't that big a deal.

Lawrence called a bunch of times after that, and we talked about the weather, about sports, about some of the crazy people on his route, about what was happening at school. Chitchat. It was better than doing homework, and it passed the time. And, honestly, the fact that he was Black made it a little daring, but it didn't go any further than that. He hinted that we should get together in person outside the pharmacy, but I wasn't interested, so we talked on the phone or when we ran into each other at the store, and that was that with Lawrence.

Meanwhile, it must have gotten around that Annie Waxman was okay talking to Black guys because, out of the blue, one day I got a call from James, one of the better basketball players on our team, a small forward who was a first-time starter that year, our junior year. I knew him through cheerleading, of course, but I had never really talked to him one-on-one. He seemed quiet to the point of aloofness, and I had other friends on the team—Bobby, who I already told you about, the point guard, and Sam, one of the top basketball players in Kentucky, who was also Black. I sat next to him in one of my classes.

On the phone James's quietness seemed more sweet than aloof. He started by saying that he had heard I talked to Black guys, but after that, I did most of the talking. I was intrigued and even a little thrilled that he called. It made a certain sense. He was a basketball player, and I was a cheerleader. If you want to get all armchair psychologist about it, my father wasn't around much, and when he was around, his crazy behavior sucked all the attention out of any room he was in, so you could say I was craving male attention. And what could be more male than a six-foot-three-inch star basketball player?

When James suggested we get together after a few phone calls, it was a different story than with Lawrence. I wanted to see him, but I knew it was risky. I played coy for a while, but that didn't last long. We decided to get together. This was February 1969.

Since Mary was in Florida for college by then, I could use the family car almost anytime I needed to. I met James at the local cemetery, where he could walk from his neighborhood to the back lot where graves hadn't been dug yet. That first time, he wore a lavender shirt and pants. "Wow," I said to myself, "that lavender is bright!" But I let it go. It was the sixties.

When I arrived, James got into the car, where we could be sure of some privacy, and we talked. Well, I talked, a lot of nonsense probably. I don't remember. It was a little awkward, actually. We knew we were crossing boundaries, and we were nervous and self-conscious. At the same time, the atmosphere between us was electric, like that feeling just before a thunderstorm. James was different. I loved the color of his skin, deep brown and very even. I wanted to touch his skin, to stroke it. It drew me in, made me feel giddy in a way I had never felt with anyone else I had dated. I must have been different to him as well, this pert little blonde cheerleader. Forbidden fruit for both of us. We leaned closer as we talked, and our hands brushed against each other. Suddenly, without really deciding, we found ourselves kissing. We made out for a while. I came up for breath and thought, *What are we doing? We've got to be careful.*

We stopped for the night, reluctantly. James walked home through the backfield, and I drove to my house, my heart beating fast. *What am I doing?* I thought for sure Mom could see the story of what had happened on my face when I got home. I chatted with her briefly, then escaped to the safety of my room to think about my time with James, to dream about what was to come.

Chapter 3

THAT NIGHT

We progressed from there. James kept calling and asking me out, and I kept saying okay. We were sixteen, with all those teenage hormones running wild. It was fun. It was exciting. It was daring. It was scary. My friend Bobby, the point guard, knew James from basketball. He has since told me he always thought of me as a huge risk-taker. I'm not sure about that—until James, I was the proverbial Good Girl—but I did know that I was having a lot of fun. Seeing James fed something in me: my need for attention and approval, to be seen as special, to put something over on my parents. After a couple of dates, I guess you could say we were boyfriend and girlfriend, though we never did anything to formalize it. He didn't give me his letter jacket or anything. How could he under the circumstances? I don't think I could say that we loved each other, but we were definitely "in love" in that way that makes teenagers a little crazy.

Since I had my own phone line, no one else really knew we were dating. We had to be very, very careful, sneaking around in a town so small. In public, we pretended we didn't know each other. For example, the big state basketball tournament was held in March. The team took a bus to Louisville, and the cheerleaders went in our own van, but we all stayed at the same hotel. James and I passed each other in the lobby and could only glance at each other with the thrill of secret longing. Grace, who was also a cheerleader, later told me she thought something might have been going on between James and me, but she wasn't going to ask me about it. She figured I would tell her when I was ready.

James and I had sex in the car fairly soon after we started seeing each other. After our first date, we had moved to the back seat to give us more room to make out. A couple dates later, James pushed to go all the way, and I went along with it.

I was a virgin, so he was my first. I know now that it was something I probably shouldn't have done so quickly, considering we hadn't been seeing each other that long. And, of course, at this time, "nice girls" weren't supposed to have sex at all. But we were on a hurtling train that would have been hard to slow down, let alone jump off. I don't remember how it felt, and I can't even remember if we used a condom. I don't remember if it hurt or if I bled. I've blocked out much of it. I remember going home and talking to Mom as if nothing had happened, then taking a long hot soak in the tub.

I wasn't naive about sex. (Okay, maybe a little.) I knew that one of my good friends, who was also a cheerleader, had gotten pregnant at fifteen and had the baby at sixteen. I knew others who became pregnant in high school too, so some people were sleeping around. I knew the mechanics of sex, but it wasn't pleasurable to me, especially those first few times. I mean, we were in the back seat of the car in the cemetery, and he was six feet, three inches, all arms and legs. It was awkward at best.

I didn't feel bad about it, though. In fact, I felt proud that I was with James. For me, it had less to do with the pleasures of sex than with being his girlfriend. If sex was what he wanted, I was all for it.

Once we began having sex, that became the center of our relationship. We barely talked once we pulled into the cemetery. We were young and fumbling our way to adulthood. I saw sex as something you did when you were in a serious relationship. I didn't examine my motives too deeply. It became a chicken-and-egg thing—we had sex because we were getting more serious, and we got more serious because we were having sex. It didn't hurt that my father would have been livid if he knew what we were doing. I was striking out at my absentee father the only way I knew how.

All this was happening very fast. I turned seventeen in June. School ended, and it was summer, and though I liked spending time with James—*craved* spending time with him—I was used to being around more people. It wasn't as if James and I could walk into the theater holding hands or grab a burger with my friends. It was very confusing for both of us. We created this little bubble that was just the two of us. It was unreal, separate from the rest of our lives. At the same time, it was what we lived for, what we thought about when we first woke up in the morning and when we went to sleep at night. I'm sure it's the same for many teenagers with their first love, but we had the added complication—and the added excitement—of the forbidden.

By that time, a rumor was going around that I might be seeing James. Looking back, I'm fairly sure that James would have bragged about me to his friends, and that's how the secret got out. Grace told me people approached her and said, "We've heard rumors about Annie." But Grace shut them down, told them it wasn't true, because that's what she wanted to believe even though she had some suspicions. Why hadn't I told her that James and I were together since she was my best friend? I don't really know. Maybe out of fear of how she would respond. Maybe to protect her. Maybe because the more secret it was, the more exciting it felt to me. All of the above?

One of the few people who knew about James was my sister Mary. I told her because I figured I could trust her, since she had had her own secret boyfriend. She said she'd keep it to herself, but that I should be careful, that I was playing with fire.

Meanwhile, I knew another girl from school named Patty, who was also secretly dating a Black guy. Since we had that in common, Patty and I became more friendly. We understood what our other friends couldn't understand—that we felt deprived of all the normal rituals of dating: going to movies, watching TV on the couch, and school dances.

That was when we got the idea to double-date, something "normal" couples did all the time. We would meet James and her guy at the Old Church, the oldest church in the county, with an interesting history. It was built in the 1790s, when the slaves of the White congregants often attended, sitting in the balcony. After emancipation, the church allowed Black people to periodically use the church for their own services; then in 1870, the White congregants built a new church and sold the Old Church to the Black members, who formed their own congregation.

But we weren't there for the history. The church was way out of town down a dirt road, and during the week it sat empty and gave us some privacy. We either lay out on a blanket or stayed in the car.

On what became forever burned in my mind as THAT DAY on July 26, 1969, I should have known something was going on because Daddy showed up at the house about the time I was heading out. Mom had thrown him out months before because he was having an affair with Nancy, his secretary, more than fifteen years younger than him, but we still saw him many weekends. He came over to give Mom a check and cook steaks for the family. He always got angry at me because I did steak wrong, according to him. I liked my steaks medium well and covered in A.1. Steak Sauce for flavor. He'd yell that I was ruining good beef. He ate his steaks nearly raw, "still mooing," as he liked to joke. As with most things with him, his way was the only way.

But this was a weeknight when he strolled in. I said to myself, *What's he doing here?* He was still there when Patty picked me up. I told everyone we were going to get ice cream at Dairy Queen, but Patty and I kept to the plan and drove straight to the church.

Once we arrived, we coupled up and started kissing and doing what seventeen-year-olds do, but after a while, we got bored. The attraction of the Old Church was its privacy but not much else. We stayed outside on a blanket, but the churchyard was overrun with field grass, stones, and brambles. We were tired of rocks poking at us through the blankets. It was no longer the romantic ideal we had imagined.

Patty's boyfriend said nobody was at his place. Why didn't we go there? We got back in the cars and drove to the guy's house in the Black part of town. The house had concrete stairs leading up to the front door. We went in, and after talking a bit, James and I went into the back bedroom, while Patty and her guy went to another bedroom. James and I were making out, fumbling at our clothes, looking forward to making love in an actual bed, even if it wasn't our own.

"Stop," I said to James. "I thought I heard someone call me."

"What?" he said. "That's crazy. No one knows we're here."

I held us still and listened but didn't hear anything else. I shrugged it off and took up where we left off.

All of a sudden somebody yelled, all in a panic, "Annie! Annie! Your daddy's here." This time I heard it loud and clear. It must have been Patty.

I scrambled to button up and straighten my skirt and blouse, scared about what was going to happen. James and I walked out of the room and found a window looking out on the front yard, and sure enough, there was Daddy, standing on the front stoop, red-faced and banging on the door with the side of his fist, yelling, "I know you're in there, Annie, goddamn it. You better get out here. If I have to come in there, I won't be responsible. Get your ass out here."

I was thinking, *Oh my God! What do we do? What do we do?* I was pacing in a weird sort of circle, running my hands through my hair. James was frozen in place, the poise and grace he showed on the basketball court deserting him.

I remembered the back door and said to James, "Go. Run. Get out of here."

"Shouldn't I—"

"Get. Just run. I'll take care of Daddy." I knew there was a good chance that if Daddy got hold of James in the heat of his rage, he'd kill him. I was his daughter. I wasn't exactly sure what he was going to do to me, but he probably wouldn't kill me. I pushed James toward the door. "Go!" Finally, he listened and took off out the back door and over the fence to the next block. This was his part of town. I figured he'd know where to go, how to stay hidden.

I took a deep breath and opened the front door. Daddy reached in, grabbed me by the arm with one hand and the neck with the other and threw me down the concrete stairs. I was wearing a miniskirt and a short-sleeved blouse. The fall scraped up my arms and legs.

"I know what you've been doing. I've had you followed all day. Get in the car."

While I was lying on the ground, crying and shaking with fear, I wondered how I had been so stupid. Of course Daddy would have me followed. Daddy's girlfriend Nancy got out of her car, marched up to me, and spit on me. Then Daddy pulled me up by the arm and threw me in the back of his car. He and Nancy had driven separately.

I noticed other cars up and down the street, some with antennas—Daddy's cop friends. That was how they tracked us.

I was slipping into shock, not even crying. As we drove home, I remember Daddy yelling the whole way, though I don't remember what he said—nothing nice, I'm sure—about what kind of girl I was and what he was going to do to me.

We turned into the driveway at the house. He got out of the car and pulled me out of the back seat where I'd been catatonic.

Mom heard the car and walked onto the screened-in porch and into the yard. She took in my messy hair and the scrapes on my legs and arms. "What is it?" she said. "What's going on?"

"She's been with a n*****," Daddy told her. "I just caught her with a n*****."

Mom screamed.

Daddy dragged me into the house by the arm and spun me to the den floor. His rage was uncontrollable. He bent over and hit me. Mom pushed Claire into the master bedroom, locked the door, and ordered her not to come out.

Mary, who was home from college, heard the noise (how could she miss it?) and walked into the den.

Daddy snarled at her. "Did you know?"

"Know what?" she said, playing innocent.

"Did you know?" he repeated.

"Yes," Mary said. She was nineteen and saw no reason to lie. It wasn't anything she had done.

"Why didn't you tell me?"

"Why would I tell you something like that?"

This didn't help my cause. Daddy was in a rage and hit me harder. And harder.

Mary yelled, "Stop it! Leave her alone. You're going to hurt her."

Instead of stopping, Daddy jerked me off the floor and threw me into an armchair. "Did you sleep with that n*****?"

Because I was too frightened to lie, I said, "Yes."

With that answer, he dove at me, gripped my neck in his two hands, and choked me.

Mary and Mom yelled for him to let go. They pried at his arms and hands, trying to pull him away. He'd let go of my neck first with one hand, then the other to swat them away, but when they ganged up on him at the same time, he took both hands off my neck, and Mom and Mary both yelled, "RUN!"

I ducked under their arms and ran out the front door. Behind me I heard someone yelling, "He's got his gun! He's got his gun!" I ran into the neighbor's backyard, expecting to be shot any second. I heard a shot go off. I flinched, but I didn't feel anything. He missed or had shot into the air. To this day, I don't know if he was trying to shoot me or scare me. It's not something we ever talked about.

After a while—I have no idea how long—I ended up back at the house. I'm not sure how. Mary probably tracked me down and led me back while Mom calmed Daddy down. I was sitting in the den next to the kitchen when the police came to the door. Mom must have called them, or perhaps a neighbor. I don't really know. It was a summer night, and all the windows were open.

The officers were my father's friends, but they also had a job to do. Two of them were talking to my father. "Now Woody, we're going to have to take your guns for a spell."

"Go ahead," he said. "I still have my fists," as he raised them to his chest.

But he did surrender his weapons, and the police were able to calm him enough so they could leave. We all tried to stay out of Daddy's way as best we could after that.

Chapter 4

THE AFTERMATH

The news traveled quickly. Relatives and other adults came by the house, even the minister of our church. Some offered my parents support. Others just gawked. Daddy was out of control, and people were concerned about what he might do. They were also curious about what had happened. The whole thing became a huge spectacle.

Daddy's brother, Uncle George, a tall, imposing tobacco farmer, arrived, came up to me, and told me I had brought great shame on the family. He didn't spit on me like Nancy had, but he pursed his lips like he wanted to. Other people took it upon themselves to tell me the same thing in different ways, over and over and over again. Everyone was talking about me and to me and at me and over me. I no longer existed as a human being. I was now The White Girl Who Had Slept with a N*****. It was a strange state of limbo. I was in a kind of shock. I don't know if it was the medical definition of shock, but I had shut down. I wasn't saying anything, and I wasn't thinking anything. I had crawled into a corner of my mind where no one could find me. It was surreal.

When it grew dark, people began to leave. That was when we noticed the parade of cars heading slowly into our cul-de-sac, driving past the house, and heading out just as slowly. There must have been more than forty of them. Later we heard that the rumor going around had been that Daddy had shot and killed me—people were calling the funeral home because they thought my body was there. They wanted to learn for themselves. Some of them gave the house the finger as they passed, yelling enlightened things like "N*****
lover!" I don't think Patty faced the same kind of treatment, but it wasn't her family who found us. The bigger the family name, the bigger the scandal.

Grace has since observed that the town treated those events like huge, juicy, gossipy entertainment, that people hounded her for every last detail because they knew she and I were friends. Grace's father warned her that she was going to get some heat from her other friends and the town at large and that she had a tough decision to make, but if there was ever a time Annie needed a friend, it was then. In fact, Grace's boyfriend pressured her to end her friendship with me—to choose him or me. She chose me and has been a steadfast friend throughout my long journey. The boyfriend eventually backed down.

Once the house emptied, Daddy turned on Mary, berating her for betraying him, Mom, and the family name. He wasn't making a lot of sense. Finally, he yelled, "You know what? You're not going back to college. After what you've done to our family, you don't go back to Florida. You're staying home."

Mary said how unfair that was. Daddy yelled that she should have told them what was going on. Mary, who until then had been on my side, flashed me a look of anger and took off to her room.

Suddenly Daddy announced he had to leave. He needed to get out for a bit, to clear his head. He got in his car and left.

Mom imagined that Daddy was going to kill himself because, you know, that was a reasonable reaction to the tragedy of his daughter sleeping with a Black man. Although she had kicked Daddy out of the house and they were separated, she was still very much in love with him and took it upon herself to save him.

Mom got in her car, leaving me with Mary and Claire, whom someone had finally let out of the bedroom.

I learned about some of this later. Mom followed Daddy, who ended up at the local steak house where he met up with Nancy—not the isolated spot where he was going to kill himself that Mom expected. As soon as Mom saw Nancy, she felt betrayed all over again, gunned the engine, and slammed into Nancy's car. Then she drove home, slung the car into the driveway, and walked with purpose into the house directly to the kitchen. There she grabbed a butcher knife and announced she was going to slit her wrists. We didn't know what to do. Not five seconds later, Daddy ran through the front door and tried to calm her down while she was crying and repeating, "I'm going to slit my wrists. I'm going to slit my wrists."

Eventually, Daddy must have calmed her down and taken the knife away from her. She didn't hurt herself, and the next thing I remember is the both of them sitting at the kitchen table over a cup of coffee like any married couple after a spat.

I lay on the couch for a while, then went into my room and fell dead asleep. Sometime later, the door slammed open, and Daddy burst into my bedroom, startling me awake. It was about two in the morning when I looked at the clock. I was groggy from sleep and swollen and sore from the beating, and I thought to myself, *Now what?* I imagined he'd been drinking because that's what he did, and that's how he was acting.

"Get up," he commanded. "Get your ass in the backyard."

I thought, *Wha-at*? I moved like a zombie.

Daddy took my bulletin board off the wall. I had pinned up articles from newspapers about the cheerleading squad and the sports teams, including some about James leading the team in scoring or winning the game on the final shot. This bulletin board was an evolving scrapbook of my life and relationships in high school, one that I could see whenever I came into my room.

I couldn't figure out why Daddy wanted the bulletin board until we got outside and he led me to the charcoal grill. He leaned the board up against one of the grill's legs, grabbed the bag of charcoal, and dumped a half a bag of briquettes into the tub. All of his movements were exaggerated with rage and drink. Then he squirted most of a can of lighter fluid onto the charcoal, struck a wooden match on a brick, and underhanded it into the grill, which lit up with a *whoosh*.

Daddy retrieved the bulletin board, ripped off one of the articles, which sent the thumbtack shooting off into the night. He handed it to me and nodded toward the fire. I shook my head. He gestured with his hand toward the fire, and when I didn't move, he cocked his arm as if to backhand me. I didn't want to get hit again, so I reluctantly laid the article on top of the fire, where it browned, curled, ignited, then blackened into ash.

We did the same with every article and picture on the board, one by one at first, then a handful at a time. I felt nothing while I watched my life burn to ash. My mind felt empty. Daddy was an overpowering force, like gravity, futile to resist. When nothing remained on the corkboard, he picked up the barbecue fork and stabbed the embers to make sure every last piece of paper had gone down in flames. As if that was going to change anything. As if that was going to somehow make up for the fact that I had been with James, that I had, in Daddy's mind, dishonored the family. With the fire shining on his face, he looked like a mad demon, and that's how

I saw him, a devil I hated at that moment with all the passion of a wronged seventeen-year-old.

The next day, I faced a court-martial of a kind. Consequences came fast in our town, especially for something as scandalous as this. On behalf of the cheerleading squad, Grace came over to collect my gear: the pom-poms, uniforms, and cheerleading jacket I had worn so proudly, that had been at the core of my identity since grade school.

I'm glad it was Grace who came.

Grace had learned about what had happened when the first alternate on the cheerleading squad had called her to ask what was going on. The cheerleading sponsor had called the alternate and told her I wasn't on the squad anymore and that she had been promoted.

Grace didn't know anything about it. She called our house, intending to talk to me, but Mom answered. Through Mom's crying and angry yelling, Grace came to understand that I had been caught with James, that I was off the cheerleading squad, and that she should come to collect the gear.

I was in Mom's bedroom when Grace arrived, and I could see Grace at the front door, but Mom wouldn't let me talk to her. I was virtually a prisoner, but I left the bedroom and got near the door where Grace could see me. Mom barely talked to Grace herself, simply yelling, "Take these! Get these out of here. She's been with a n*****. She's never going back to that school with those people." Then she threw the pile of gear at Grace, one item at a time. Grace remembers seeing me sobbing and looking like a zombie; I remember feeling as if I had been banished from the kingdom, as if everything I loved was being stripped away.

The day after Grace came to the house, Daddy returned, and he and Mom woke me up. I could see the morning light through the half-opened curtain. Daddy did most of the talking. He commanded me to pack some clothes.

"Where are we going?" I mumbled, still half asleep and not thinking clearly.

"We're taking you to the hospital," he said. "You need some rest."

Daddy had talked to Dr. Rankin, our family doctor, who told him I was having some kind of breakdown and needed to go to the hospital.

I was definitely out of it, that much I knew, so I did what they said: packed some clothes for a couple of days—I don't know how many—and we went to the hospital in the bigger city nearby. Daddy drove. Mom rode up front with Daddy, so distraught she had taken Valium to calm down. I was in the back seat, not understanding what was happening, not caring.

We arrived at the hospital. Things got even blurrier from there.

Dad parked up front. We got out of the car and entered the elevator. I remember wondering where they were taking me. I watched the elevator lights flash as we went up. We didn't stop until the top floor, where the doors rattled open. Across the tiny lobby, I saw thick windows embedded with wire and a set of solid-looking doors that appeared to be locked.

"Where are you putting me? Where am I going?" I screeched suddenly and turned to run away just as the elevator doors rolled shut.

Daddy twisted me back toward the locked doors. "You need some rest," he said. "It's for your own good."

My parents walked up to the windows, pulling me with them, and pressed a button, which set off a buzzer. Male attendants with thick arms, dressed in scrubs and tennis shoes, appeared from behind a closed door and let us into a little room off the lobby. The door locked shut behind us. Another locked door led to the rest of the ward.

A large blonde woman dressed like the others held a clipboard with papers attached while she asked my parents questions, ignoring me completely. I was seventeen and had no legal standing.

I clutched my suitcase as if it were a life raft. Then she handed my parents the paperwork to sign, each in turn, and that was that. I was checked into the hospital's psychiatric ward. Mom gave me a hug but wouldn't look at me. Dad glared at me and said, "You know we're doing this because we love you."

This is what you call love? I remember thinking while trying to control the urge to spit in his face, like Nancy had in mine. I felt such anger, pure rage, the kind of anger only he was usually allowed to feel, a hatred I had never felt before.

I barely noticed when they left.

Another large woman, this one with brassy red hair, entered through the locked door holding a Dixie cup of water and a tiny pill cup pleated on the sides. She gave me the pills first, then water, and without a word made sure I swallowed them. She led me to another small room on the other side of the door and handed me a cardboard box and a stack of clothing that turned out to be scrub-like pajamas and a gown. So much for the suitcase of clothes I had packed, which I realized was no longer with me.

Once I saw the woman wasn't leaving the room, I turned my back to her, changed into the hospital clothes, folded my street clothes very neatly, and placed them in the box. Someone who folded clothes that neatly couldn't be crazy, right?

Once I changed, I was put in a room with four twin beds, only two occupied. One of my roommates was an eighteen-year-old alcoholic. I knew this because she offered me orange juice and vodka from a thermos. I have no idea how she smuggled that in. She was very thin, her hair flat and brown, her eyes shiny and red-rimmed. I declined.

Our other roommate had recently butchered her husband. I don't remember how I knew that—I must have found out later. She was strapped down to her bed and didn't have much to say, as she was heavily drugged, dead to the world, not showing that spark of life even sleeping people have.

And there I was with the two of them, and I still don't know why. Sure, I was a bit out of it, sobbing almost constantly, and stunned by all that had happened so quickly—my father having me followed, his rage and brutality, the screaming and yelling, the beatings, getting shot at, my mother's hysterics. I hadn't had much time to process what was happening, let alone understand it.

This was all I could come up with when I thought about it later, when I think about it now. Such was the deep-seated racism in my family and the town that the only explanation for me seeing James was that I wasn't right in the head, that I had lost my marbles, that I was crazy, literally insane. It was also a clever cover for the family—*It's not us, no sir, it's her. She's nuts. Why else would she do such a thing?* (Another girl in town dated a Black football player about the same time I dated James. Her mother had recently died, so "they"—the townsfolk—attributed her actions to her mother's death. She had lost her mind with grief and didn't know what she was doing, they explained. Because, you know, "No one in their right mind . . .").

My parents mentioned that the doctor had said something about sending me to the hospital for protection. But who was the doctor trying to protect me from? My boyfriend or my gun-crazy, alcoholic father from his own worst inclinations? Maybe a little of both. I don't know. Nobody was asking me how I felt. I got the impression that my feelings were the last thing that mattered to anyone. It was all about how it looked, about what people thought.

In fact, I don't remember talking to a psychiatrist or attending anything resembling therapy the whole time I was in the hospital. All I remember were the pills, morning, noon, and night, and how they made me feel like I was walking through a heavy fog, thick and opaque. I don't know what pills they gave me, and I don't know why. Because I dated a Black guy? That seemed to be justification enough.

I don't remember much else about my stay there. Deeper into the ward—I thought of it as a huge maze—was a common room filled with card tables. When we weren't in our rooms sleeping off the effects of the drugs, we sat at the card tables. That's where we ate our meals, stared at the other ill people in the room, and sometimes actually played cards. All I remember is feeling fuzzy-headed and saying over and over to myself, *What am I doing here? What am I doing here? What am I doing here?* Some of my fellow patients had legitimate conditions that needed treatment, and all I had done was date a Black guy. Daddy was the one who should have been in there, not me. I had never suffered from any mental health issues. I had been a pretty happy kid, under the circumstances.

I was there for about a week, I think. I don't remember having visitors. Grace later told me that she had visited but that I wasn't really myself, that I didn't really want to talk about anything with anyone. I don't remember her visit at all. Bobby sent me flowers and a card. I realize now how brave they both were to reach out to me, since I was considered radioactive by the rest of the town.

The next time my parents showed up at the hospital was to take me home. At least that's how I remember it. I reversed the process with the clothing and the rooms. To release me, my parents signed different papers on a clipboard with a different nurse, and that was that. I don't know why they released me. Was I cured? Did the doctors decide I hadn't really needed to be there in the first place? Had my parents only wanted to scare me? Get me out of the way until things blew over? I'll never know.

The ride home was silent. My father said something about hoping I'd learned my lesson, but then even he went quiet. This was a relief. I didn't want anything to do with either of them just then, and the silence allowed me to stay safely inside my head.

I hadn't heard from James while I was in the hospital. I hadn't expected to, and I couldn't blame him. I heard through the grapevine that Daddy and his buddies were looking for him, and that when they found him, Daddy was going to kill him, so James went into hiding, and I'm sure it wasn't easy. It was hard enough being Black in our town without a target on your back, and here James had my father, a big man in town, out to avenge his family's honor.

At home, they left me little time to lick my wounds. A few days after I returned, Mom, Mary, Claire, and I set out for Florida to move Mary back home. They were sticking to their guns in punishing Mary for not informing on me and James.

That was a miserable drive, all 850 miles there and 850 miles back. Mom was in a nasty mood and spent most of the time berating me for the shame I had brought on the family. Mary wasn't really talking to me at this point, since I was to blame for the miserable car ride and her punishment. Claire was eight years old, and all she did was whine for attention, which no one really wanted to give her. We all had problems of our own.

We finally arrived in Florida and packed Mary in a huff—none of us wanted to be there. The ride home was less of a strain, but only because we were all wiped out and kept to ourselves, each of us locked up in our anger at the world.

When we arrived home, another surprise waited for me. I wouldn't be going back to the public high school for senior year. My parents had decided this without consulting me. Instead, they were sending me to a Catholic boarding school in North Carolina, known for straightening out bad girls like me.

I was shocked at first. *How can they do this to me? They're so unfair.* But the more I thought about it, the more relieved I was that I'd be getting away, that I wouldn't have to face the town or my parents for all of senior year.

It turned out to be the best thing for me.

Chapter 5

NEW BEGINNINGS

Taking my senior year at the boarding school instead of my old public high school was the best thing for me for two reasons: one practical, the other emotional.

The practical reason was that I had become a pariah, an outsider, an outcast, and if I had tried to go back to our public high school for senior year, I would have been ostracized and literally spat on. I soon realized that the trip to Florida had been as much to get me— and the rest of the family—out of town until the uproar died down as it had been to move Mary out of the dorm. Once we returned, I couldn't drive around town, even for simple errands. The couple of times I tried, the people who recognized me rolled down their windows, gave me the finger, and yelled vile things at me. N***** lover. Slut. Whore. Even though I expected a negative reaction, the sheer force of their rage and hatred staggered me. I was essentially the same person I had always been, except now they knew I had been dating James, a young Black man, whom, by the way, they had been more than happy to cheer for when he was winning basketball games for the high school.

Here's how strong and far-reaching the consequences became because of the small-minded townspeople. Eight years later—almost a full decade—when my sister Claire was sixteen, she was refused admission to the high school sorority because of what I had done and the "stain" I had left on our family's name, though I had been long gone by then.

I lay low at home for the rest of the summer—about four weeks. This is when I lost my belief in God and religion. Until then, I had been religious in the way many kids are. I wore a cross on a chain. I said my prayers at night and brief prayers throughout the day. I went to church most Sundays with Mom and my sisters. But I reconsidered my faith after the church folk, the very same ones who professed to believe in the Bible with its teaching to "love thy neighbor as thyself," abandoned me and worse—turned on me in hatred and called me vile names. So much for "God is love." Their hatred wasn't Christianity as I knew it. I lost faith in any sense of a loving God looking over me.

I hadn't seen or talked to James since the day my father caught us, and I had no intention of doing so. I was busy trying to please my family to the extent that was still possible, and I also didn't want to put James in greater danger.

Later in the summer, some of the cheerleading squad sent me cards showing their support. "Just a little something to let you know we'll always be here if you need us." Grace and another friend signed a card that said, "What can we say at a time like this? I guess, 'Goodbye, good luck, and we'll miss ya is good enough. So go down to North Carolina, hold your head high, and they'll love ya!'" The cards were very touching, considering that many other people in the town had nothing good to say about me. Thinking about their support today still brings tears to my eyes.

That was when it hit me how much my life had changed in just a few weeks. Later, Grace told me she wondered if my mother actually blamed the cheerleading squad for leading me astray, that Mom might have thought that the other cheerleaders were bad influences, that if I hadn't been a cheerleader, none of this would have happened because I never would have been that close to the basketball players. In fact, Grace thought that it might have been my mother who called Mrs. Jones, the cheerleading sponsor, to tell her I'd no longer be on the squad.

According to Grace and Bobby, they were both mercilessly interrogated by friends, family, and nosy town gossips about what had happened to me, but they stayed loyal and didn't give in to the gossipmongers, just stated the facts as they knew them—that I had been secretly dating James and that after my father had caught us, my parents were sending me to boarding school. Personally, though, they said it felt as if I had died. One minute I was in their lives, their close friend. The next I was gone, like I had fallen off the face of the earth.

ⓢ ⓢ ⓢ

The boarding school sat on a hill encircled by a brick wall with a locked iron gate at the entrance. The campus spooled out from the old Victorian mansion at its center, and the school had the feel of a medieval convent, which made sense, since it was founded as a Catholic convent school in the early 1900s, although it had always accepted students of all denominations.

The boarding school has since merged with a coed day school, but back then it was an all-girls school that took both boarding and day students. As a result, the school had a split personality. Most of the day students were local kids who wanted to get a strong, private school education. The boarding program, on the other hand, had a reputation for taking in girls who had gotten into trouble—drugs, shoplifting, sex, running away—and helping them get back on track. I'm sure that's what appealed to my parents. That, and the fact that the school wasn't anywhere near where we lived.

Toward the end of my time there, I had an interesting conversation with the sister who was head of school. She said, "Your father never told us why you were sent here, just that you'd be trouble, so I should keep an eye on you. But you've been the kindest, sweetest, nicest girl. I'm curious. What was it? Why were you sent here? You don't have to say if you don't want to."

But I wanted to. If I was going to be an accidental rebel, I wanted people to know why. The more people who knew the truth, the more they would understand, and that would lessen the stigma. You could argue that there shouldn't have been a stigma in the first place, but that's an argument from another time because, believe me, back then there was a stigma. When I told Sister the story, she was stunned. "I'm happy you came to be a student here, but that seems somewhat . . . extreme. We aren't racists here."

And though I agreed that my parents' reaction seemed extreme, I was glad to be at the boarding school. I hated my parents, hated them for what they had done to me—for what they were still doing. This was not a teenager being a drama queen. I truly hated my parents. Being almost three hundred miles and two states away from them in North Carolina was the best thing for me—for us all, really. The distance helped me heal and grow stronger, to become emotionally healthier, to think of myself as an individual separate from the Waxman tribe and its chief. I had room to breathe at the new school, without my parents, who had been acting more like prison guards, watching my every move, waiting for me to screw up so they could come down hard on me. Despite the fact that the school was locked up tight at night and we couldn't go off campus without permission, I felt freer there than I had felt my entire life at home. I felt safe there. I felt like my own person.

The school had many rules and routines, but I learned to enjoy the structure. For one, we had to wear uniforms during the day. I came to love the uniforms. You didn't have to worry about what you were going to wear, which saved time in the mornings. You had knee socks, shoes, a skirt, and a vest—and that was all. Since everyone wore the same thing, there was none of the fashion competition of a typical public high school. I found that refreshing. And because it was an all-girls school, there was no competition for the attention of guys either. We only met guys at the school dances or other events we shared with some of the all-boys prep schools in the area. The one I remember best was an Episcopal school on a beautiful campus in the Blue Ridge Mountains.

We went to classes during the day, of course. French class stood out, not because I remember any of the language—I really don't—but because the teacher was open and friendly. She wasn't a nun. She wasn't even Catholic. She was of the Baha'i faith and very tolerant of the differences of others. I ended up telling her about James and me, and she was a very supportive listener. One of the tenets of the Baha'i faith, as I understand it, is that marriages between different races are a path to a more peaceful world. Given my own experience at home, I had my doubts about that. But my French teacher lent a sympathetic ear and encouraged me to live my own life.

After school we all had to stay busy and involved—everyone was required to join in one or more of the extracurricular activities offered. I took horseback riding and competed in walk-and-trot tournaments. I took lifesaving classes, and I was on the swim team. At night after dinner, we studied quietly in our rooms with the doors open while the nuns did the rounds to make sure we were at our desks at least pretending to do homework. I remember that the work was challenging but not impossible. Without all the social activities of a public high school, we had plenty of time to get it done.

Every day we followed the same schedule: wake-up call, clean up and get dressed, breakfast, classes, lunch, classes, after-school activities, dinner, study hall, clean up and get ready for bed, and lights out. We had about a half hour of free time between dinner and study hall that we could stretch out if we ate fast, and a few minutes after classes.

We could only go into town on the weekends, and only with permission. The administrators kept money that our parents provided for us in the school "bank." We took some out when we went into town, where we let loose a little, buying ice cream, soda, and candy and doing any small personal shopping we needed.

Despite all the sneaking around I had done previously in high school, the whole time I was at the boarding school, I never tried to go off on my own, never tried to break curfew or break any of the other rules meant to keep us safe. This is what my parents didn't understand. I wasn't really a bad girl, a juvenile delinquent, as we used to say. I hadn't done anything that teenage girls in love against their parents' wishes hadn't been doing forever. Except James was Black, and to my family and the town, that put me on par with drug addicts. In fact, in anger, my parents actually told me once that it would have been better if I had been on drugs instead of with a Black guy. I didn't really know what to say to that.

I grew close to my roommate Debbie, who came home with me for Thanksgiving that year. We flew in, and Mom picked us up at the airport.

Mom was well-behaved because we had company, and Daddy didn't really live at the house anymore. Mom did it up for Thanksgiving dinner, with a huge turkey and all the fixings. Mary and Claire were there, and Daddy came for dinner, then went to Nancy's.

Debbie and I had fun, and it was good to get outside the gates of the school for a while. Grace visited at some point over the weekend and met Debbie. Mixing my two worlds—my roommate from boarding school and my family and friends in Kentucky—was surreal, and I think it cushioned me from the sting of returning home. Southern hospitality prevailed—everyone was on their best behavior.

Debbie had come from a much more liberal family and had been shocked by my story when I first told her at school. She was surprised again when she visited by how nice everyone was, how we seemed like a normal, loving family. I didn't know what she expected. White hoods and burning crosses? It showed how complex, multifaceted, and, yes, even hypocritical people can be when it comes to family.

ᔕ ᔕ ᔕ

At boarding school, I wrote James a letter. I felt safe and free in a place where my parents couldn't censor my mail. And James wrote me back.

He was surprised to get my letter. He didn't think he'd ever hear from me again. He didn't think I'd *want* to see him after what I'd been through. We didn't get too deeply into the details of what had happened, but we did write that we still cared for each other and wanted to be in each other's lives. He told me going back to school for senior year had been tough for him. People had been nasty, adults and students both, but having grown up Black in Kentucky, he was used to it. (His family—his mother, brother, sister, and father, who never lived with them but lived five houses down—didn't have the money to send him to an out-of-town school the way mine did.) He said he had been more worried about me than about himself, with all the threats my father had made. I assured him I was okay and enjoying my time at the new school. I was relieved that I didn't have to face all the hateful, racist people back home, and I felt bad that he had to.

When I went home for Christmas, I grew brazen. I told Mom I needed to run an errand and borrowed the family car. I went to a pay phone on Main Street and called James, and we met in the cemetery for about ten minutes. We hugged and held each other, but that was about all the time we could risk. I did realize, though, that no matter what my parents had put me through, it wasn't going to keep me away from James. It had done the opposite. It made me want to see him even more. It had turned me into an accidental rebel. I was out to prove something. *You think you're going to end this?* I challenged my parents in my head. *I'll show you. This will never end with us apart.*

James and I continued to write for the rest of the school year, both of us looking forward to graduation.

Our boarding school graduation ceremony was a formal affair. My parents still attended family functions together and drove down from Kentucky. Claire and Mary did not come. We graduates wore long white dresses and gloves up to our elbows and carried red roses as we walked across the stage to pick up our diplomas and shake hands with the head of school.

My parents were relieved that my year at boarding school had gone so well and felt justified in their decision to send me there.

Then we packed the car with my stuff and headed home. On our way out, we saw a young Black man and a young White woman from the school get into a car together. My parents' eyes went wide with surprise. They had sent me to boarding school to keep me away from just that sort of thing, and here it was happening right in front of their eyes! It seemed like the perfect ending, an odd and ironic punctuation to my year of exile in boarding school.

Our ride home was filled with chitchat. We avoided any talk of why I had been at boarding school. We pretended as if it had never happened.

Chapter 6

BREAKING AWAY

At boarding school, we all applied to college whether we were planning to go or not. But I knew from my experience there that I was better off away from home and the family, so there was no way I wasn't going to college. My father insisted that all his daughters were going to college, and we understood he'd be paying for it. Buying stuff for people had always been his love language.

I wanted to get out of Kentucky, so I applied to the University of Tennessee but didn't get in. I was a B and C student, and I had never been interested in academics. That was Mary, the straight-A student. I got into a state university in the western region of the state, though, and that's where I decided to go. I looked forward to being on my own.

James received a scholarship to play basketball at a private college not far from our town.

According to Bobby, his high school teammate, James came into his own as a basketball player in his senior year of high school.

James began the season as a decent high school player, but ended it as a player worthy of a scholarship. Bobby attributes some of that to me—that because James had been dating me, his self-confidence and drive had grown. Bobby thought that because White people in the community were watching James so closely, he was motivated by their surveillance to be the best basketball player he could and prove to them that he was "worthy" of me and our relationship.

That summer before college was uneventful. Mom and Daddy kept me busy, too busy to see James. Daddy got me a job at a real estate company, where I filed and did other tasks. He bought me a new Ford Pinto to drive to the office, but I totaled it in two weeks. He bought another car to replace it, a silver Mustang II. We went to the lot together to pick it out. I asked him if it looked good with my long blonde hair. He laughed and said it did and paid for the new car. I thought it was the least he could do after the way he had treated me, and as a teenager at the time, I didn't feel even the remotest bit guilty accepting it.

I was a pariah to most of the people in town, who still gave me the finger when I was out driving, or rudely stared me down, sneering in superiority. But I wasn't a hermit. Mary was gone for the summer, working as a waitress in the Grand Tetons, but I remember going out with friends, Bobby and Grace and some of the others from the cheerleading squad.

Grace's father continued to support her friendship with me, saying that I was still Grace's friend and that she should be there for me. Grace's mother, on the other hand, struggled with what had happened. "Are you doing that too?" was her mom's first question after she learned I was caught with James. She was anxious about what people might think because Grace was my friend, afraid of humiliation for her own family. Later in life, when Grace's mom was dying of ALS and couldn't communicate any other way, she typed out an apology on a ticker tape: "When Annie and James got caught,

I wasn't there for you or Annie." It was one of the regrets of her life, she confessed. This was almost twenty-five years later, when Grace and I were nearly forty. That guilt had weighed on her mother that long.

I saw James once toward the end of summer very briefly. I have no memory of how we arranged it. It wasn't by my phone, since Daddy had pulled our private line out of the wall the summer before. I had been to Myrtle Beach with Grace and my family, and I had a really dark tan. James and I put our arms side by side to compare. "We almost match," James joked. (My mother thought I was too dark, of course.) He said he missed me—that he missed us. I told him I missed us too. My parents were watching me like a hawk, however, and I was trying to get my life back on track, so I didn't think it would be a great idea to get together more than that one time. He took my lead on that, but his face fell in disappointment.

§ § §

I moved into my college dorm in the fall of 1970.

In college, I embraced the rebel nature I apparently had inherited from Daddy. Daddy had always been the black sheep of the Waxman family, and many people told me I was just like him—social, outgoing, and stubborn. I looked more like Mom, though.

The early seventies were an extension of the sixties, and I took full advantage of these new liberties. Free from my parents and small-town busybodies, I took risks. I did crazy things. I partied hard, drinking and smoking pot, sneaking into men's dorms, looking for excitement and love in all the wrong places.

I borrowed Daddy's car one time for a spring break trip to Florida. The girls who came with me were into pills and pot. We must have had $10,000 worth of drugs in the trunk. I wasn't into pills, but I did smoke pot. I smoked so much on that trip that I really don't remember much about it. (What's that saying about the seventies? If you remember it, you weren't really there.)

My biggest rebellion was getting back with James, and it was *not* so accidental this time. We had been exchanging letters since senior year of high school, and maybe because we were off the leash at college, the letters became more intense. I remember in one letter James wrote how much he missed me and loved me and begged to get back together. That letter included his telephone number, which he had retraced several times to make the numbers stand out. Soon after that I called him, the old feelings returned, and we got back together, picking up where we left off, including sneaking around and hiding what we were to each other. My father had moved to the city by then, not far from where James's school was located. We still weren't able to bring our love into the open.

James couldn't really come to see me because he didn't have a car, and his time was taken up with basketball. My college was a bit of a suitcase school that emptied out on the weekends. I could almost always get a ride from people heading James's way if I pitched in for gas. I sneaked into James's dorm many times, usually staying the whole weekend.

James had a Black roommate at college named Evan who was also a basketball player. When I came from my university to see James on the weekends, Evan looked out in the hallway to make sure it was clear for James to bring me in. Their room was on the first floor and not far from the dorm entrance. I would literally run straight to their room. Evan would stay in another player's room when I visited.

On the weekend, James always had basketball practice and games as well, so he was gone a lot. There also had to be time for studying. James was a good student and on full scholarship, so he had to keep up his grades, which meant he needed time to study. While waiting to spend time with him, I'd study myself, watch TV, and sometimes smoke a little pot. Then when James had a break, he'd head to his dorm room, often bringing snacks or chips—anything to curb my hunger pains until he could get fast food for us for dinner.

Using the bathroom in the boys' dorm was quite another feat. James would get other basketball players that knew we were together (and knew I was visiting) to be on the lookout for me to go to a stall. I had to go fast—preferably during the night or early morning when fewer people roamed the halls. Honestly, at times, I desperately needed to go, and on a few occasions, I just peed in a bucket.

We couldn't leave the room together, so we stayed in, watching TV, drinking, smoking pot, and making love. It was a strange, isolated existence, intense excitement followed by deadly boredom.

When I couldn't get a ride somewhere, I hitchhiked the interstates, especially when I visited Bobby at Vanderbilt in Nashville. A lot of people traveled that way then. It was the early seventies, remember, a real hippie time. I wore my hair straight and long with a headband to keep it out of my eyes. I dressed in jeans and a suede jacket with fringe hanging from the sleeves and moccasins on my feet. My shoulder bag was also fringed and suede. I held my sign out at the entrance ramp to flag down a semi. The drivers didn't mind the company, though sometimes they expected more than conversation. I tried to be talkative and engaging to keep their minds off other things. I kept a hammer in my bag for protection, which I gripped while riding in the trucks.

One guy scared me pretty badly. "You're so pretty," he leered. "I don't think I'm going to drop you off." I grew afraid. I remember trying to be really nice, to talk to him in a soothing voice about how I needed to get where I was going, or a lot of people would miss me. To my relief, he eventually let me out at my exit, and with my heart pounding, I got away from his rig as fast as I could. I learned my lesson. I never hitchhiked on the interstates after that, though I sometimes hitchhiked around town.

Looking back, going to see James was pretty bold, since my father lived nearby. In college, I liked to take things to the edge. We had to be very careful, and I think the risk was part of the thrill, that we were putting something over on my father. At the same time, we kept a low profile. The city was huge compared to our hometown, but Daddy was well-known in business circles there as well. I didn't go to James's games because I didn't want to risk being recognized by someone Daddy knew.

Very few people knew that James and I were together. James's basketball coach was one of them. I don't know how or why he knew. We also spent some time with Dan, one of the White basketball players, and his White girlfriend. We didn't go out. We just hung out in their apartment, but it was a break from James's room.

∽ ∽ ∽

James and I continued in this way for most of freshman year. We saw each other every few weeks and slept together, using condoms or the withdrawal method for birth control, since James didn't like condoms—no guy liked condoms. Sometimes he claimed he didn't have any. The pill had come out in the early sixties, but doctors weren't very open to giving the pill to young girls. Numerous complications could happen. I went along, as I did with many things back then. Love, lust, call it what you will. I didn't question it, didn't even think much about it. That's the way it was. When you're young and in love, the passion just takes over, and the guy is supposed to pull out in time. Yes, it sounds ridiculous now, but that's the method we tried to use. James would say, "I promise I can pull out in time!" I remember telling him, "You *must* do it." Then sometime in the spring I was late with my period and feeling a little queasy. I bought a home pregnancy test, and sure enough, I was pregnant.

I was in a panic. I could never have a child with James without my father trying to harm me or James or both of us. In fact, I didn't feel any connection to this baby inside me. It just felt like a mass of cells to me. It didn't feel real. But I did feel afraid of what my father would do and what my family would say. Although I had rebelled against my family by dating James, I wasn't strong enough to break away from them completely. I wasn't ready to be totally on my own.

Without too much thought, I decided to have an abortion. I was nineteen, a freshman in college, with my whole life ahead of me, too young to have a child, no longer religious. I became an accidental rebel again, not out of any deep-held philosophical belief about women's rights to abortion but out of necessity. And because I had that choice. Isn't that what abortion rights are all about? Choice? Choice without judgment? I made a mistake, got pregnant when I didn't want to be pregnant, and I had a choice: to have the baby or have an abortion. I chose abortion, and I have no regrets. Did I take the easy way out, as some have accused me? Believe me, there's nothing easy about getting an abortion. Besides, that's not really for others to say. They don't get a vote. That's freedom of choice. At least it used to be.

I called my sister Mary, who had transferred to another university by then. Sobbing and gasping for breath, I told her what happened. Mary came through for me, even though as kids we had fought a lot. We were only two years apart, but we didn't have much in common. She was the smart one, more studious. I was the popular one, more social and outgoing. She thought I had it easy because I was cute, and everybody liked me. Mary was very attractive herself, but she lacked self-confidence. I thought she had it easy because she always got A's, and our teachers always seemed to like *her*. She played an instrument and ended up in the band, a very different high school experience from mine.

I'll never forget the year we were in French class together. She had decided to take French as a junior while I had started as a freshman. She sat behind me. On a typical school day her friends picked her up for school, and of course she couldn't have her little sister tagging along. I had to take the bus or have Mom drive me.

Once she was gone, as revenge, I would ransack the clothes in her closet. One time I wore her pink mohair sweater, one of her favorites. When I arrived at first-period French class, she was already in her seat. I strutted into the classroom, sashayed past her, and sat in my seat in front of hers, knowing that as soon as she saw the sweater, she'd go ballistic.

Once class started, she poked at me with her pen when the teacher wasn't looking, pulled my hair, and whispered that she was going to kill me when we got home. Later at home, we fought like dogs after the same bone, pulling hair and kicking each other in the legs and wherever else we could reach. Mom had to rush in to break us up while we protested loudly about who started what and who stole whose clothes.

But when I needed help with that abortion, Mary was the one who pulled it together. The state of New York was one of the few states in the country where abortion was legal in 1971. (Although, if abortion hadn't been legal in New York, I would have figured out how to have an illegal abortion. That's how firm I was in my decision.) Mary called in many favors to scrape the money together for me to fly from Nashville to New York City and pay for the procedure once I got there. (Nashville was closer to my college than the airport in Lexington, and I was less likely to run into anyone who knew me there.)

Before I went to New York, I told James I was pregnant and getting an abortion. Like many guys at the time, he shut down and wouldn't talk about it. It was up to me to figure out. He didn't offer to go with me to New York because that would have been impossible, and he didn't offer money toward the costs of the trip and the procedure because he didn't have much extra. I wouldn't have taken it from him anyway. I gave most of the spending money Daddy gave me to James because James didn't have much, and it was another way for me, a young rebel, to get back at Daddy.

Because I was terrified and dazed, I asked my girlfriend Donna to go with me. Mary put up the money to pay her way as well. This was not a pleasure trip, so we took a cab from the airport directly to the clinic, which was on 73rd Street, I remember. It was a no-frills brick building, a little on the dingy side. Inside, the changing rooms were cramped and stuffy, and the procedure rooms were only big enough for the stirrup table and maybe two people to move around.

The other patients in the waiting room seemed to be from all over the country, so I didn't feel too out of place with my Kentucky accent. The aides who conducted me through the process were professional and neutral, if a little stern. I don't really recall many of the details. I was going through the motions, and if Donna hadn't been there to say, "This must be it," "Fill out this paperwork," "Go into that room to change," and so on, I don't know if I would have been able to make it through.

The procedure itself went quickly. They gave me pills to relax, but I don't think they worked because I was far from relaxed as they set me up in the stirrups. Once they put me under, I don't remember anything until I woke up sitting in a reclining chair next to Donna in post-op. When the attendants saw I was awake, they gave me some pads for the bleeding, handed me the plastic bag with my clothes, and told me to get dressed. And that was that. We found another taxi and headed back to the airport.

I had lost a lot of blood, so I didn't feel well. I flew back to Cincinnati, which is closer to our town than Nashville, thinking maybe I'd just go home for a while to rest. Donna kept on to our school. I ended up getting a ride home. I don't know by whom or how. Once I got to Mom's house, I pretended I had just arrived from school, that I wasn't feeling well, and that I needed a break. (That much was true.)

I set myself up on the couch with a blanket and a hot water bottle to rest and watch TV, still cramping and bleeding. I took aspirin every few hours for the pain.

I had been there for a while, zoning out, when Daddy came over. I remember thinking that was odd since Mom and Daddy were still separated. But maybe he'd heard I was home and wanted to stop by.

Mom always made a great potato salad. She offered some to Daddy, who accepted. Then she said to me, "Come on up and have some potato salad. You've got to eat something."

My father was watching me closely, as if studying me. To get him to stop, I untangled the blanket and pushed myself up from the couch, groaning. I felt as if someone had kicked me in the stomach with sharp-toed boots. I shuffled to the table and sat down. Mom put a small bowl of potato salad in front of me along with a fork.

I wasn't that hungry, but I took a forkful to be polite.

Daddy stared at me, which made me nervous. I had spent the previous year avoiding his attention. I tried to ignore him and looked to Mom to start some small talk, but she was fussing at the sink. To distract myself, I brought the forkful of potato salad to my mouth, and just as I was about to taste it, Daddy said, "I know you had an abortion in New York yesterday."

I dropped the fork and looked down at the table, defeated and ashamed. He always had a knack for catching me off guard. Did he know everything I did? Would I ever be able to get away from him?

He took my reaction as confirmation, then said, "Was it Black or White?"

He acted as if that was the most important detail, not how I was feeling, or whether I had lost too much blood, or if I had thought about keeping the child.

"White," I said, without hesitating. What else could I say after he had already tried to kill me once? I lied to protect myself, and I lied to protect James. It was a matter of survival, and I don't regret it.

"Whose was it?" he said with the persistence of a police interrogator.

For a second, I thought about saying it was none of his business, but that wouldn't have gone over well and would have prolonged an already painful situation. Besides, he was paying for college, and I never could say no to him.

But I could lie to him. I named a guy from school I had dated a few times when James and I weren't exclusive. He was a cute hippie type with long hair named Ron, who drove a hearse with a peace sign on the roof. We'd drive to concerts, get stoned, and sleep in the back of the hearse, which was done up as a bedroom. One concert I remember was Crosby, Stills, Nash & Young in Nashville. I asked my parents for permission to go, and they said no. I went with Ron anyway. We slept in the hearse overnight after the concert.

"You know I'm going to find him and kill him," Daddy said matter-of-factly, as if informing us it might rain later.

Oh shit, here we go again, I said to myself. *Now there are two guys my father wants to kill because of me.*

Mom was doing something in the kitchen, her mouth twitching with disgust at my insult to her Catholic sensibilities.

We know now that Daddy never made good on those threats to kill more than one of my boyfriends, but here's the thing about Daddy—you believed that he *could* do it, if he chose to, that if he didn't do it, it was because he had decided not to, not because he *wouldn't*. Daddy was scary that way. He liked to put fear in people to show how powerful he was.

Remember, Daddy sometimes operated in the gray areas of the law. And here's a weird thing he said to me that day. "You should have just told me about [the pregnancy]. I could have taken care of it." He must have arranged abortions in the past, maybe even for some of the women he fooled around with. For once I was glad that he hadn't come to my rescue.

Daddy must have been keeping an eye on me even when I was away. I don't think he had me tailed twenty-four hours a day or anything like that (otherwise he would have known that James and I were back together), but he knew people everywhere, friends and relatives, people who owed him favors, and they must have kept him informed of my doings and whereabouts.

It wasn't only me Daddy was keeping an eye on. James told me in one of his letters that every once in a while he'd see one of Daddy's company cars circling the block near his dorm, "Waxman Homes" written boldly on the door. That could have been a coincidence since Daddy built many homes in the city, but I didn't think so. He was so blatant about it. I'm sure Daddy wanted James to know he was out there, watching, waiting. This was intimidation, not surveillance.

ᔕ   ᔕ   ᔕ

When I returned to school for the end of the term, then for the summer, James and I picked up where we left off. James always stayed at school over the summers to work out with the basketball team, so to spend time with James and avoid going home, where I'd feel like a prisoner again, I always found a reason to take summer classes too.

James and I saw each other and slept together when it suited us, but we didn't talk much about anything that mattered, like the abortion. The feelings James wouldn't talk about in person sometimes came out in his letters, though. In one letter from August 1971, he took issue with a comment I had made in my previous letter about the abortion. He quoted what I wrote: "It doesn't matter what it was. It's dead now. We have to go forward." He must have asked if I knew whether it was a boy or a girl. He wrote how my answer hurt him, that it seemed flip, as if I didn't care, and then went on to say that "a part of me and you had to die because of our love, and [our love] could not survive any other way." That was pretty deep for James, and I was moved. I even felt a little guilty—not about following through on the abortion, there was no way to avoid that—but in my youth, I hadn't considered what James might have felt about it.

We were on again, off again during this time. When I read through our letters, I see that we argued a lot, often about who was seeing whom. In one of the letters, I told him that we were broken up and I was dating other Black guys. He didn't like hearing that. He had a double standard. What was okay for him—being with other people—wasn't okay for me, especially if they were other Black guys. He wanted to be the only one.

I sure knew how to pick them. I dated another Black guy freshman or sophomore year. He was light-skinned with a big Afro, a very good-looking guy who drove a sporty Fiat. We rode in the Fiat through the campus and town with the top down, my long blonde hair blowing behind us. One night we went to his apartment to smoke pot, and I don't know if the pot was laced with something or what happened, but all of a sudden, he pulled a gun on me and started yelling like a crazy man, nothing I could really understand. To this day, I have no idea what set him off. He pointed the gun at me and threatened to shoot me, and I was like, "What the hell? What are you doing?" I talked him into putting the gun down. Once it seemed safe, I took off. I doubt I saw him again after that, but such were the times that I honestly don't remember.

James wasn't the only one who had a problem with me dating Black guys. I often hung out with the football players at school. One night a few other women and I were having dinner in the dining hall with some of the football players, most of them White. We were sitting at one of those long tables they have in dining halls, and opposite me was this White guy from Philadelphia, the salt and pepper shakers between us. I was chatting with my friends like we did, about who was dating whom. Most of the team and the other women knew I was dating some of the Black football players. It wasn't really a secret. In mid-sentence, I turned my head toward this guy from Philadelphia, and all of a sudden I got a face full of pepper.

"Why'd you do that?" I said, jumping to my feet and brushing the pepper from my face, coughing to clear the flakes from my throat. He had unscrewed the lid of the pepper shaker and thrown most of the contents in my face. My eyes and nose watered, and my tongue burned.

"White guys aren't good enough for you?" he taunted.

Apparently some of the White guys took it personally that I was dating Black guys, as if I was rejecting them, as if it was some kind of comment on their manhood, as if I was saying they didn't measure up somehow, as if I was cheating them (and cheating *on* them), that I should be dating them instead. And throwing pepper in my face was the way to win me over? Acts and comments like these were driven by a racial contempt that still astounded me despite my experience back home.

I was caught between two worlds and didn't fit well in either one. Every time James and I broke up, he sweet-talked me into going out with him again. He brought out the big guns. "I love you so much. I miss you. I've never loved anyone as much as I love you. I won't ever hurt you again. I didn't really care for that girl. It was just for fun. You're the only one I care about."

I fell for it every time.

I fell for it because I loved him, or at least I thought I did, and I fell for it because I had something to prove—to my friends, to my parents, to the world, and most of all, to myself. If James and I broke up for good, that meant everyone else had been right, that we shouldn't have been together in the first place.

We'd show them.

Chapter 7

TOGETHER AT LAST

That's how we spent our college years: on again, off again, each living our own lives during the week and getting together most weekends.

My degree was in elementary education. I planned to teach elementary school. Many relatives on my father's side were teachers, and since I couldn't think of anything else I wanted to study, that's what I chose as well. I just wanted a degree. James studied physical education, but let's face it, he was at college to play basketball, and he did that very well. He lettered all four years, and when he graduated, he was the school's career scoring leader. (Today, almost fifty years later, he's still number four on the all-time list. He was that good.) Three of the years he played, the team won twenty or more games, and his senior year (1974), he was the school's Athlete of the Year across all sports. For these accomplishments, he was inducted into the school's Hall of Fame.

Once we graduated from college, James got a job teaching physical education in an elementary school and another job as a head basketball coach at a small university.

We moved in together. As with most of our decisions as a couple, we didn't have any big, formal discussion about it. We just did it. Our main concern was making sure Daddy didn't know about it, but that wasn't difficult because Daddy lived about an hour-and-a-half away and had businesses out of state as well. He was busy with his own life and work and not concentrating on me for a change.

Meanwhile, I was having trouble finding a teaching job even with the help of my father, with all his connections. The job market was tight that year, and finally Daddy said, "Sorry Sweetie, I just can't do it. There are no jobs out there."

I didn't mind, actually. I had majored in education by default, and my experience as a student teacher in a first-grade class was not fulfilling. I was graded well by the mentor teacher (despite one day crashing into her car on the ramp to the highway), but I learned that teaching children was not my thing. I didn't really like kids that much. I didn't like teaching. I wasn't crafty enough to create bulletin boards and fun activities and all that stuff children love.

I still had to get a job, though, and I was having trouble figuring out what kinds of jobs to apply for. I didn't want to work in a restaurant or store. Then it hit me. When I was doing errands, I often passed a health spa, which offered fitness and aerobics classes, in addition to other kinds of spa activities like saunas and massages. I had been a cheerleader, I told myself. I could teach those classes.

One day I got up my nerve and walked into the spa. I asked to speak to the owner and wouldn't take no for an answer. (I knew that much from watching Daddy all those years.) When I finally got in to see the manager, I asked him if he needed a good instructor and told him about the state competitions our cheerleading squad had won. He looked me up and down. I was cute. I had kept myself in good shape by exercising every day, and once I talked to people, they usually liked me. He hired me on the spot.

For the two years James and I lived in Kentucky, I was an aerobics instructor and trainer, working with twentysomethings trying to stay in shape and thirty-, forty-, fifty-, and even sixty-somethings trying to get back into shape. I enjoyed that job, and I was always positive and encouraging. It was engaging without being taxing, and I dealt with people every day, not lesson plans or bulletin boards or paperwork. It was the perfect first job for me. I am sociable, and I like people. I even got some sales experience. If a potential customer seemed reluctant to sign up, the owner brought them to one of my classes. My enthusiasm often won the day.

Those two years living together were a pretty good patch for me and James. We lived in a mixed-ethnic neighborhood. We spent much of our time socializing in the Black community, the bars and restaurants there, and the clubs, where we would dance all night and drink Colt 45s. We had people over to our place, mostly Black friends.

We both drank a lot in those days and smoked pot because we were on our own and we could, but also, I think, because of the stress of being secretly together. Daddy had business in our city every so often. We never knew if we'd come across him or one of his cronies. We were constantly on edge. We drank to take the edge off.

I got happy when I was drinking, but James got mean. He'd pick on me and criticize me in a nasty voice. If I had been healthier myself, I would have seen this as the red flag it was, but I was used to this kind of behavior from my father. It was nothing new. In fact, it was familiar, even comfortable, so I let it go.

I met James's family one time at their home in the Black section of town. His mother was a big woman, tall, which was likely where James got his height. She was a strong woman, and proud, but also kind. She cleaned houses for a living. He had a younger brother and sister, whom he was fairly close to. They were poor, but they seemed to get by.

James and I were young and on our own, enjoying our new-found freedom. We never talked about what had happened to us in high school. We were both shut down and never really talked about anything too deep. I remember watching TV while I plaited James's hair. Some kind of sport was always on when we were home, especially basketball. James taught me how to plait his hair properly. He had a pretty big Afro, the style at the time, and I would go section by section, putting Vaseline on the hair, then weaving the strands together. It took a couple of hours. He would keep it in for a day or two, then he'd take it out. It kept his hair from getting dry and gave it more body. Braiding James's hair was also an intimate ritual that brought us closer together. It helped me feel like I was part of the Black community. In many ways, I was more comfortable in the Black community than James was in the White community, even though sometimes I was the only White woman in sight. The Black women didn't always appreciate me, but it never came to violence as it might have the other way around. Many Black women were understandably suspicious and critical of me, though.

Before moving to Los Angeles, James and I would occasionally go to a late-night club like a speakeasy in downtown Louisville. I was most often the only White girl there. Many Black women didn't acknowledge me at that bar. I tried to ignore this because, on some level, I understood why they would ignore me—I didn't belong. A Black girlfriend of mine in my college dorm told me, "A White woman dating a Black man doesn't sit right with Black women. It makes them feel like they're not good enough for the Black man." I knew something about that already, but I wasn't going to give James up just because other women didn't like me for it, and I naively hoped I could win them over. I was so nice, after all.

Another time when we were living in Los Angeles, I met a Black couple from James's work. Marcus and his wife Roberta had us over on a Saturday afternoon. They lived in a well-to-do Black area in LA. The guys went to play basketball, but I stayed behind with Roberta. We planned to join them later. I remember feeling somewhat uncomfortable with her and the way she asked questions about our relationship, like she was interrogating me. As usual, I tried to stay upbeat and nice.

"Why'd you move to LA?" she asked.

"We had to escape the backward thinking in Kentucky."

"How long have you been together?"

"Since high school."

I told her some of our history—that we'd been in LA for about five months. At that point, though, I could tell from the tone of her questions that she was wary and didn't care for me. I was a White woman dating a Black man.

After we got in her Jaguar to go meet the guys playing at the park, she began driving very fast and erratically, even running stop signs through the street.

"Please slow down," I said. "You're scaring me!"

She didn't care. She just kept driving fast on surface streets. Her questions at their home, followed by her aggressive driving, made it obvious to me that she didn't like me and wanted to frighten me. Once we arrived at the park, I refused to ever get in the car with her again.

Personally, I came to LA to escape judgments about my relationship, naively thinking California was some kind of utopia, especially regarding interracial couples and race in general. I was wrong. I ended up learning the hard way that I was wrong about a lot of things.

For example, James had been a famous high school and college basketball player in Central Kentucky, and I had taken him off the market. At least I thought I had taken him off the market.

The problem was James hadn't taken himself off the market. I found this out the hard way.

One day I came home from the spa at lunch. I don't remember why. Maybe I had forgotten something, or maybe I just needed a break. I went into the bathroom, and there was another woman's lipstick and powder sitting on the sink. I dashed into the bedroom. The sheets on the bed I had made before I left that morning were all crumpled and messy and not in a taking-a-nap kind of way.

I sat on the couch, shocked and angry, taking it all in. In college, we had both slept with other people, but now that we lived together, I thought that had all stopped. At least it had for me.

James, who was still in the apartment, was surprised to see me. His eyes twitched guiltily toward the bedroom. I confronted him immediately. "What's going on here? What is this?" I waved the lipstick in his face. "What is this?"

He explained that the woman who belonged to the cosmetics worked at the same elementary school he did. She was getting a divorce and was very upset. She needed someone to talk to. He brought her home to comfort her and, well, they didn't mean to; things kind of just happened . . . or some such nonsense. "Things just happened": the cheater's mantra. It would never happen again . . . just as he had written in his college letters.

I was furious. I flipped out, crying and yelling, saying how could he do this to me? But eventually, I let it go. I stayed with him through that betrayal and moved with him to LA. I was on this march. James and I were going to work out, come hell or high water.

James's messing around may have been a mixed blessing. It gave me the strength and the leverage to act on something I had been thinking about since college graduation—getting out of Kentucky.

As she did with many things in our lives, my sister Mary took the lead. She and her husband William left Kentucky first. They had been married since 1972, when she was twenty-two, having met the summer before when they worked together at a resort in Florida. They decided to take a trip out West, and after they returned, they were going to live together, they proudly announced. With her German directness and rectitude, Mom said, "Well, you better be married when you come back because you're not living in sin around here." On their return home, they called Mom's bluff, stopped in Vegas, and got married.

They settled nearby, where Mary and William both worked for our father. Daddy wanted them to work like he did, to be available all hours of the day. He'd show up at their door late at night, drunk and talking all kinds of nonsense. Mary knew enough not to let him in, but he'd bang on the door and yell about ungrateful children and what they owed him. This was stressful for Mary and William, not to mention inconsiderate of their neighbors.

Mary and William were willing to work hard, but at the end of the day, they wanted to go home and leave work at work. Daddy was actually grooming William to take over the company, but William and Mary wanted no part of that, figuring they'd never have a moment's peace. They decided to move out of state. William's parents had retired to Arizona, and Mary and William had liked it there when they visited them on their western swing. They moved to Arizona and have lived there ever since.

Even once Mary and William left, Mary and I talked often. Never one to hold back, she asked me why I couldn't do the same thing. My life in Kentucky was no way to live, she argued, hiding my boyfriend from our parents, living in fear that one day Daddy would find out and hurt us both—or worse. "What do you want for your life?" she asked me. "What are you going to do? You can't live there and stay sane. Where are you going to go?"

Mary got me thinking about it seriously, so seriously that I began to plan the move. I wanted to live somewhere exciting, somewhere big, somewhere I could lose myself and find myself at the same time. New York City or Los Angeles, then—the Big Apple or Hollywood. But New York had bad memories from the abortion. I had also spent some time there on a field trip when I was at boarding school, and I didn't like the closed-in feeling of all those people and skyscrapers. I'm from Kentucky. I lived on a farm when I was a kid. I wanted more open space. Los Angeles it was.

To check it out, I flew to Arizona, stayed one night with Mary and William, and booked a ticket to Los Angeles. After I landed, I got a taxi and had the driver show me the highlights of the city: Venice Beach, the Original Farmers Market, Rodeo Drive in Beverly Hills. He drove me around for about four hours. Then I took a flight back to Arizona and spent a little more time with Mary and William. When I arrived home, I told James, "Quit your job. We're moving to LA in August."

"What?" he said. "Why?"

James didn't want to leave. He had lived in Kentucky all his life. He was comfortable in Kentucky. He had two good jobs. We had made good friends. His family was still in town. My father was too busy to bug us much. Things were fine. Why did we need to leave?

We were both young. I'm not sure I explained it well to him. Looking back, what I think I wanted to say was something like, *I'm tired of living a secret life. I want to live out in the open. I don't want to be looking over my shoulder for my father or one of his cronies. I want to get away from Kentucky small-town life, where everybody is up in your business, and "family," no matter how screwed up, comes before anything else. I want to put it all behind me and set myself—set us both—free.*

What I said instead was, "I'm leaving in August with or without you. Quit your job. Don't quit your job. I don't care. I'm done here."

James was never a big talker, so he didn't tell me what arguments he made with himself pro and con. But one night while we were watching TV, he turned to me and said, "I'm going to resign from both my jobs."

"Okay, good," I said.

And the next day he did.

Chapter 8

CALIFORNIA DREAMING

We rolled into Los Angeles, California, during rush hour on August 8, 1976, pulling a U-Haul with my silver Mustang II, wondering what we'd been thinking. Cars were bumper to bumper, Mercedes and beaters alike, in four, six, eight lanes of traffic. We had never seen anything like it in Kentucky. Drivers in the far left lane would zip across three lanes in front of us to get to the exit, but no one would let us change lanes when we put on our turn signal. I was sure some distracted driver was going to take out our U-Haul any second. It was petrifying. James's eyes were wide, and his hands were tense on the steering wheel.

Before we left, I had gone home to pick up a few last things from the house. I was eager to leave, but I still got teary-eyed when I said goodbye to Mom and Claire and the house in which I had lived most of my life and so much had happened. Daddy was also there to send me off. He thought I was driving out West with a girlfriend and gave me a gun for protection, a pistol of some kind. My parents weren't happy that I was leaving, but they were resigned to it. Like any concerned parents, they told me to be sure to take good care of myself.

I drove to our apartment, picked up James, and we headed across the country, taking turns at the wheel. We talked about sports and listened to the radio. We played music cassettes (we both loved soul music) and Richard Pryor's comedy tapes. We talked about the promise of LA, where we wanted to live, and what we faced ahead of us. We received many stares for our Kentucky license plate and the fact that James was Black and I was White. When we tired of the road, usually late at night, we took our chances with motels that weren't too far off the interstate and had outdoor entrances to the rooms with no lobbies to walk through. I would go in by myself and reserve the room because I had the credit card. James would park the car around back, then follow me to our room once I gave him the all clear.

Filling up on gasoline was a little trickier. Some stations wouldn't give us service because we were a mixed couple, and we'd have to move on to the next stop. Once we figured that out, we always kept enough gas in the tank to make it to the next stop and the next one after that if we had to. After a few close calls, we figured out a new plan. When we rolled into a gas station, I hid on the floor in the back under a blanket so it looked like James was alone. The last thing we wanted was to get stranded on the highway. That would have been all kinds of trouble.

Can you imagine turning down paying customers just because one was Black and one White?

In LA we found a Holiday Inn that let us register, then ordered Jack Daniel's and room service. We sat out on the balcony and looked out on the city. It was smoggy from all the traffic, and the air had a chemical taste. What had we gotten ourselves into?

From where we sat, we could see the pool. James noticed a number of Black people swimming. "This place must be a dump," he said, standing up abruptly. "Let's get out of here."

"Are you serious? We're going to pack up and go to another hotel?"

"Yes, I'm serious. I'm not comfortable here."

So we packed up and went to the parking lot where we got in our car with a little U-Haul on the back, and we went to another Holiday Inn in the heart of Downtown LA.

At the time, I found James's reaction confusing, although not necessarily surprising. He didn't communicate well with me what he thought or felt throughout our relationship. This experience seemed like a hard reminder of the prejudice and implicit bias James grew up with in Kentucky. Perhaps he felt we wouldn't be accepted as an interracial couple. Everything was unknown as we arrived in LA. I think maybe he felt he was protecting me when he saw all those Black people in the pool, or maybe this was an expression of his own internalized racism against Black people. LA was known to be more accepting of different cultures, but it was also new territory for him. Perhaps after twenty-five years of wariness and fear, James was going to take some time to adjust.

After a few days, we moved into an apartment in Mid City with a mixed-ethnic group of tenants. Within a couple of weeks after that move, I started to feel sick to my stomach. I bought a home pregnancy test, and sure enough, I was pregnant again. I had been on the pill since the first abortion. (Mary had made sure of that.) But I didn't like the way it made me feel. A few weeks before we left, I had been fitted for a diaphragm by a doctor who made it clear to me that he thought I shouldn't be having sex. Then I went off the pill, but obviously the diaphragm had not been fitted properly (or we didn't use it correctly). I figured I was about five weeks along. I had driven all the way from Kentucky without even knowing I was pregnant.

I couldn't have that baby either, for all the same reasons. We had just rolled into LA. Although we were older (both of us twenty-four), my family still wouldn't have approved. My father may very well have tried to hurt us again, and I still wasn't ready to be a mother. I had come to LA to reinvent myself, and having a child wouldn't let me do that.

I'd felt stuck in Kentucky, hiding and unable to live with confidence and freedom, waiting for the next disaster to happen. Moving to LA opened a new world for me, for us. I could be free to explore possibilities. I could feel more comfortable in my relationship with James, able to see through eyes not clouded by fear. It was liberating, not perfect, but still liberating. In fact, I knew I would be moving to California with or without James. I'd become tired of living under this veil of secrecy and fear. I knew LA wouldn't be a paradise, but it offered a new and exciting place to find out exactly who I was and what I was capable of.

When I was working as a trainer and aerobics instructor in Kentucky, a woman there knew a producer in LA. She'd sent him a message that I was coming out. I thought maybe I could do commercials, be a different person, not be frightened about where I was going—reinvent myself as a person who didn't have to fear how people saw me.

Having a child would wreck my plans and take away my freedom. At that time, I also didn't really like children, which I'd discovered during my college elementary education classes. Besides, James and I didn't have jobs yet. We lived in an apartment. We didn't have much money, just the $3,000 I had brought with us. We weren't ready for children. We weren't ready to be parents.

When I took the test, James and I were in the apartment together. We were probably drinking, since we had nothing else to do.

I showed him the result.

He took another drink, then grunted.

"Here we go again," I said.

We didn't talk about it in any great detail—we didn't talk about anything important in those days. We were both shutdown after what we'd been through in Kentucky, but we both knew what we had to do. Another abortion.

I was angry that I had gotten pregnant a second time. I remember feeling pissed at myself, thinking, *This is* not *supposed to have happened. I swore I would* never *have another abortion.* But here I was again, the Bad Girl. I had been treated as the Bad Girl back in high school when Dad caught me with James. I thought I had gotten past that by moving to California. I wanted all that bad feeling to go away. Like so many women, I was taking all the responsibility for birth control and blamed only myself for getting pregnant again.

This time James drove to the appointment, a place in Inglewood sponsored by Planned Parenthood. James sat stiffly in a waiting room chair, his long legs splayed in the aisle, while I filled out the paperwork and paid up front with some of the $3,000 I had brought with us to California. This facility was newer and cleaner than the one I remembered from New York, and the doctors and nurses were more blandly polite in that way I came to associate with California.

We sat in silence until a nurse holding a clipboard called me into the examination room. She handed me a hospital gown and indicated I should change. I stripped out of my clothes, put them in a plastic bag with a drawstring, and put on the gown with that embarrassing opening in the back. The nurse patted the examination table. I hopped onto the table backward and arranged myself on my back. I waited that way for a few minutes. The doctor came in, gave me a twilight anesthesia, and the procedure was done.

Afterward I felt some cramping. I rested for a bit. The attendant handed me my bag of clothes, then left me to gingerly dress myself. I walked slowly out of the back rooms, signed the release papers, and walked myself to the Mustang, James trailing behind me, eyes on the ground.

I let myself into the car. (James was never much for courtly gestures.). Then he let himself in on his side. We drove back to the apartment and drank for the rest of the night.

⑤ ⑤ ⑤

Sometime after the abortion, I found out that James had had a son with a woman he had been seeing as a senior in high school when I was at boarding school. I found out because the boy, who was now five or six, had written James a letter from Florida, where his mother had taken him after James had abandoned them.

I wasn't happy that he had kept the boy's existence from me, but I suggested he respond to the child and send him money.

He said, "I already have."

Apparently, he had his own ghosts. I wasn't happy about that child—not only that it had happened, but also that he had kept it from me. What else had he kept from me?

⑤ ⑤ ⑤

As with many young people moving to LA, I had some hopes of doing film or TV work, maybe in commercials—nothing too big. But who knew what could come of it?

A woman at the spa back home knew a producer in Hollywood, so I had hired a photographer before we left Kentucky to put together a portfolio. Once we got settled in Los Angeles, I made an appointment with the producer, and because we only had one car, James drove me there—reluctantly—because he was angry. He didn't want me to do it. He didn't want me to do anything that put me out there, that put me in front of other people. He wanted to keep me to himself. He also didn't want me to do anything at which I might outshine him, but I didn't figure that out until later.

The appointment was not a great success. I had a very heavy Kentucky accent, which wouldn't have gone over big in commercials. But the producer was kind. He suggested I try something in photo work and gave me some tips about what to do next and what to add to my portfolio.

James stayed angry and nasty about it on the drive home. "Who do you think you are?" he said. "You're not that pretty."

When we got home, he gave me the silent treatment as he often did when he was angry. This is how he punished me. He made it hard to live with him for the next couple of weeks. I'd come home from work, and he'd already be drinking and watching TV with an impervious stare. "What are you up for, for dinner?" I might ask, but I might as well not have been there. He didn't answer me or acknowledge that I was there in any way—no eye or hand movements, no expression on his face, no changes in breathing.

I soon gave up the idea of acting in commercials. It wasn't worth the anger and isolation. I'm a social person. I need human contact to live as much as I need air to breathe. I was withering away in the face of his weaponized silence. One day I told him, "I've decided not to do the acting. It sounds like a lot of work, and there are no guarantees."

The next day the silence thawed, as it always did eventually, once I gave in. He asked me, "Wanna get a drink?"

"Yeah, that'd be good," I said.

I just had to wait him out when he was in these moods. I was used to that with Daddy.

It wasn't until I got into therapy that I saw the cycle and my part in letting it happen. I had thought that was how men were, and I just had to put up with it like my mother had put up with my father. This was the thing about my mother. With all that my father put her through—the disappearing for days and weeks at a time, the cheating, the drinking, the yelling—she wouldn't let us say a word against him. That's what I knew about intimate relationships: The man could do whatever he wanted, and the woman would offer him steadfast devotion. The very definition of codependence.

I often wondered what might have happened if I had tried harder with the acting. Maybe nothing, but I'll never know. I'm sure my desire to keep James happy cut off many avenues of achievement for me. There's nothing wrong with pleasing your partner in a healthy way, where you both support each other. But when you start saying to yourself, "Nope, I can't do that because my partner won't like it," or even worse, "My partner won't let me do that," that's when it's gone too far. That's when you find yourself in a controlling relationship.

Since we didn't have jobs lined up when we left Kentucky, we both signed up with an employment agency. James decided to try something other than coaching and teaching and landed a job with an insurance agency. I got a job as a receptionist with an interior design firm, answering the phone and talking to clients. I could do that! They hired me in part because I had a college degree, but mostly, I think, because I had a southern accent they thought their callers would find attractive.

I always was an exemplary employee, conscientious and good with people. I worked as a receptionist for a while, and I got to know most of the customers and employees who walked through the door. That's how I met my next boss Harry, who owned a sales rep firm that sold office furniture to designers like the one I worked for and hired me for a sales position. I worked in the showroom at first with him and his wife Doris, who was the showroom manager. I did well there, so I was promoted to outside sales. We represented manufacturers of office furniture and panel systems (room dividers and office cubicles). Harry and Doris were an older couple, very kind, and they supported my relationship with James, perhaps because they were Jewish and had experienced their own discrimination.

I covered Arizona and Southern California, including Santa Barbara, and I loved it. I was on the road all the time. To keep in touch with the office and our customers, we had beepers at first. When we got beeped, we had to find a phone booth or borrow a phone to return the call. Later we had some of the first car phones when they came out, and then the first cell phones, which were the size of a brick.

I loved the work. It was very exciting, very social, and I've always loved talking to people. I took people out to lunch. We went out for cocktails in the evening. I brought lunch into the offices and gave presentations to architect, design, and engineering firms—anyone who could use our products. I was a great sales rep because people liked me. I was very service-oriented, and if I didn't know some of the details about a product (which happened more than I'd like to admit), I'd find out and get back to the clients. I was always responsive. There's a saying about sales that you're really just selling yourself, and, boy, was that true for me.

The insurance company James worked for had its offices in one of the high-rises in Midtown, near MacArthur Park. James worked on the operations side of things, rather than sales, and eventually became a supervisor. That's where he met Henry and Willis, who became our good friends. Both of them were Black, Henry from Mississippi, Willis from Louisiana. Henry's wife Mary was from Trinidad. She became my best friend in LA. She died of cancer a few years ago, and I miss her terribly. The group of us hung out together, traveled together, shared meals, listened to music, and went dancing. We were all rabid Laker fans, so we watched a lot of sports together at one of our homes or in sports bars.

A weird thing happened before we became close friends, though. I didn't meet Henry and Willis right away. James had told me about them, and I assumed he had told them about me as well. One night after work I was picking James up from one of their company functions. I looked forward to meeting his new friends. When I drove up to the curb in my silver Mustang, James was standing in a group of people I assumed were his friends. I put my flashers on, jumped out of the car, put my arm through James's, and gave him a kiss on the cheek—he didn't really like much PDA—and looked around the group expectantly, waiting for an introduction.

His friends stared at me like I had dropped out of the sky. Apparently, James had failed to mention that I was White. Being who I am, I quickly broke the ice, and they recovered from their surprise.

Later at home, I asked James what that had been all about. He shrugged and mumbled something about it not coming up in conversation. What? I told him it damn well should have come up in conversation—wasn't I important to him? Was he ashamed of me? Was he afraid of what people would think?

Of course I was important to him, he told me.

When I pressed him further, trying to express how much he had hurt me, he said he didn't want to talk about it. That was his go-to response for anything that made him uncomfortable. When he dug in his heels like that, though, there was nothing much I could do. When he shut down, he shut down tight.

Looking back and after years of therapy, I wonder now if James was simply afraid of the dangers of being in a still somewhat taboo relationship with a White woman, and whether consciously or subconsciously, he held back because of that. Despite some of the advances of the Civil Rights movement in the 1960s, violence against Black people, especially Black men, had not disappeared, not even close. It had been only about twenty years since fourteen-year-old Emmett Till had been lynched for allegedly flirting with a White woman.[4] Further, one of the last reported lynchings was that of nineteen-year-old Michael Donald,[5] which didn't occur until March 1981, well after James and I had first gotten together (and divorced). Donald, a Black teenager, had been chosen at random for reprisal by members of the Ku Klux Klan after a hung jury failed to convict a Black man being tried for murder of a White police-man. Then there are the more recent deaths of Black men at the hands of law enforcement: Eric Garner in New York (July 17, 2014); Michael Brown in Ferguson, Missouri (August 9, 2014); Philando Castile in Minneapolis–Saint Paul metropolitan area (July 6, 2016); and George Floyd in Minneapolis (May 25, 2020).

Since I was a White woman, I sometimes forgot how dangerous it could be to be a Black man in the United States in the seven-ties and after. My own father had made very credible threats to kill James, enough to put James in virtual hiding for a year. If some-one was going to face violence for our being together, it was likely James. Sure, I had to deal with people flipping me off, spitting at me, and shunning me (and sometimes my family), but James was in danger of real physical violence. I didn't truly understand that danger. As a young White woman, I wanted what I wanted, which was for James to treat me the way I thought I deserved to be treated, first as his girlfriend, then as his wife. I didn't see the predicament that expectation put him in, the cognitive dissonance between who we were to each other in private and the uncertainty at best, and often abhorrence at worst, about our relationship to the public at large. James bore the brunt of that, and it was nothing either of us was equipped to talk about.

---

[4] "History of Lynching in America," NAACP, accessed September 19, 2024, https://naacp.org/find-resources/history-explained/history-lynching-america.

[5] Erin Blakemore, "The 1981 Lynching that Bankrupted an Alabama KKK," *History*, updated February 5, 2019, https://www.history.com/news/kkk-lynching-mother-justice.

James may also have faced heat from other Black folks as well. The old "Who-do-you-think-you-are?" and "Aren't-we-good-enough-for-you?" argument. As a White woman, I had sometimes faced similar questions, especially in college.

Since James held everything in, he likely would have felt all these pressures as a smoldering anger. He wouldn't have been able to talk about these things, let alone "work through" them. He was secretive. He didn't tell anybody much of anything, including his male friends. Instead, he'd take his unnamed anger out on me, his clueless blonde girlfriend. On some level, he must have thought all these volcanic feelings were my fault because he was with me, though he couldn't say all that directly. He picked at me instead.

James didn't like it when I talked loudly and drew attention to myself. I love people. I love being the center of attention. I like dressing up. I *am* blonde (naturally back then!), and I love flirting. I love telling stories, a trait I picked up from my father, but my stories didn't always have a point. Some people, like James, took this to be silly and superficial, mere chitchat, that I talked just to hear myself talk. James would call me out, making fun of me when I misspoke or got things mixed up. I mean, I wasn't speaking in front of the Supreme Court. We were just having fun.

James often tried to put me in my place in other ways as well. I was in my twenties when we were together in Los Angeles, young and good-looking, I was told. James had to dig to find something to criticize about my body, but he did. He told me he hated my feet, that my feet were ugly. He'd make these claw hands when he talked about my feet to show how ugly he thought they were. He criticized my breasts as well—I don't have the breasts of a pinup, by any means—calling me a skinny White girl with nothing to hold on to. He tried to bring me down. Was he afraid of losing me? Maybe. But I think it was more a way of showing who was boss. I may have been a privileged White woman out in the broader world, but in this relationship, he was the man; he was in charge. He didn't really *say* that, but he acted that way. I didn't leave because I felt like I had to finish what I started with James—to prove that all the drama and turmoil we'd been through was worth it.

∽ ∽ ∽

Not all the time though. Those first couple of years in LA were another pretty good patch for James and me once we got past the abortion. We had good jobs. We had good friends. We went out often and had a lot of fun. We smoked pot and drank, and because neither of us really liked to cook, for breakfast we went to a diner a few blocks from our apartment near the beach, and for dinner we went to a Mexican restaurant and ate tacos and drank Margaritas.

But even in these good times, there were hints of things to come. He never wanted to hold hands while we walked, and if I grabbed his arm, he'd shake me off. He'd shush me if I talked too loudly. Sometimes he ignored me in public as if I wasn't there. I know he probably felt exposed and vulnerable as a Black man with a White woman, but this was LA—mixed race couples were not that rare.

Grace visited a few times from Kentucky, both with her husband and by herself, and she observed that things were pretty good with James and me. When James called home, I sometimes talked to his sister or brother, nothing profound, simply chatting. They all liked me. James's sister visited us for four or five days at one point, and we took her to Disneyland.

But something was still missing. We talked about getting married "someday," but James shut down any serious talk about marriage. Neither of us addressed the elephant in the room. I was twenty-six years old. I had moved to LA when I was twenty-four to be free, to reinvent myself, but I didn't feel free or reinvented. I felt like the same old Annie with the same old weight on my shoulders.

I was still hiding. I was still keeping secrets. I was still living a lie by not telling Mom and Daddy that James and I were living together in LA—that we were together at all. "Living in sin," my parents would have called it. I didn't want to deal with their condemnation. Keeping secrets is draining. It can take every bit of life out of you. All your emotional energy goes into hiding, into keeping that secret. How could we get married under those terms?

Mary knew about James, and maybe Claire did too, but when Mom or Dad called and James was in the house, I put my index finger up to my mouth to shush him and twisted my fingers for him to turn up the volume on the TV. In the actual conversation with my parents, I had to make sure I said "I" instead of "we," and if I did say "we," I had to make sure they understood I was talking about a girlfriend or a random guy friend. If they asked me who I was dating, I said, "Nobody special."

I flat-out lied to them.

Dad was too busy with his businesses to visit, but not long after we moved to LA, Mom moved to Arizona to get out of small-town Kentucky for a new start and to be near Mary and William. Los Angeles is not that far away from Arizona, so she visited several times. When she did, James had to move out. We scrambled to erase James's presence from the apartment, throwing his things in boxes and stuffing them in the back of the closet while he crashed at a friend's house. This was not healthy. I know that now. However, I was still invested in my parents' approval. I was still looking over my shoulder, if not physically, as I had in Kentucky, then emotionally. I felt like I was sneaking around, still locked in the past. Who's going to find out? What's going to trip me up? What's going to give me away? It's a very stressful way to live.

I was sick of hiding—literally, it was making me sick. I was jumpy and anxious, and I often had that nervous feeling in the pit of my stomach, like I was going to throw up. On impulse one day,

I decided to tell my parents. I didn't really think it over or talk it out with James, who was shocked when I told him. His eyes got kind of big, and he started playing with his goatee like he'd do when he was stressed. Knowing James, he probably thought, *What the fuck did you do?* I just did it. Again, without thinking of the possible consequences for James. I mean, my father had threatened to kill him when we were in high school.

This is never going to happen again, I thought to myself. *It's not right that James has to move out every time my parents visit*. I was still hiding. James moved in with a good friend of ours willingly, but the emotional burden of lying all the time became too much for me. I couldn't lie any more.

Oddly it was Mom who reacted badly when I told my parents that James and I were living together. I told them each separately, of course, as they were divorced by now, but at around the same time. I told Mom I was sick of hiding and that James and I were together in LA. She went silent on the other end of the phone, hung up, and didn't talk to me for eight months.

I think she was angrier that I had kept this secret from her than that I was back with James, a Black man, though I'm sure that being back with James had something to do with it as well. She was always worried about what the neighbors would think, which was not uncommon in her generation. And for Mom, it was even more important. As an outsider herself, having been born in Germany of Polish descent, she was particularly careful about not making waves in our small town. She wanted us to be the perfect American family.

In general, I was really bad at keeping secrets. I was an open book. My family used to joke, "Tele-gram, tele-phone, tele-Annie." If you wanted anybody to know anything, you told me, so the fact that I had worked so hard to keep this secret for at least eight years crushed Mom. It was a "what-else-has-she-been-hiding?" moment.

Mom felt hurt and betrayed, I'm sure. I didn't want to hurt her, but I also didn't want to live a lie anymore.

Daddy, on the other hand, was thrilled when I told him, a huge shock to me and James. If I had put money on it, I would have guessed that Mom would have been the accepting one, and Dad would have lost it. That's not how it happened.

When I called Daddy, I told him pretty much the same thing I told Mom: that I was sick of hiding and that James and I were together in Los Angeles.

He paused for a second; then in that direct, gruff way of his, he said, "Are you getting married?" Just like that. He didn't run down James; he didn't run down Black people; he didn't run me down. He just said, "Are you getting married?" implying, of course, that that would be a good idea.

"I don't know," I said. "We've kind of talked about it."

"When?" he said, ignoring the "I don't know" part of my response.

"I don't know," I said again, sounding wishy-washy even to myself.

"I'm paying, so don't worry about that. Let's see . . ." I heard him flipping through a calendar. "I've got some time coming up in July. We'll do it then."

I never could say no to Daddy. He had that magic gift of acting as if what he wanted was going to happen no matter what, and people usually fell in line due to the sheer force of his personality and will. This was why he was such a good businessman and such a pain in the ass sometimes.

People ask me why Daddy changed his mind about me and James so suddenly.

The short answer is I don't know. Daddy and I never talked about it.

The longer answer might be, and a lot of this is guessing, that Daddy's attitude about race had changed with the times. His second wife Nancy was more than fifteen years younger than he was and worked in government. She likely brought home more progressive attitudes about race, even though she had been the one to spit on me that day Daddy and she had found me with James. Maybe that had been just to impress Daddy. I don't know.

I also think that Daddy missed me, and this may have been even more important. We hadn't talked that much in the previous ten years. James and I were adults now. We had been together all this time, and Daddy most likely just kind of shrugged and said, "What the hell. They seem to be in it for the long haul, so let's make an honest woman out of her." There was still an element of control there—a large element—the patriarch marrying off his daughter to preserve the family honor. He had decided that was best, and since he had decided, that was that. There was no question in his mind that I wouldn't comply.

How did I respond to all this? With relief, honestly, as if a bag of sand had been lifted off my shoulders. Relief that I no longer had to keep James a secret. Relief that Daddy had responded so well. Relief that the decision had been taken out of my hands. Relief that Daddy had come through for me. It's what I had been waiting for all along.

It was settled. After all the years James and I had been together, and all the threats Daddy had made against James, Daddy was the one who decided it was time we got married.

Soon after that call, I sat James down and told him, "It's time. We're getting married."

James freaked out, not just about the suddenness of the wedding, but also that he would have to face up to the man who had threatened to kill him more than once.

"Don't worry about that," I told him. "It's Daddy's idea. He's paying."

James hesitated still, but once Daddy got involved, events moved beyond me and James, and we were just along for the ride. Looking back, I'm sure James felt he couldn't say no even if he wanted to. It would have been next to impossible to resist the force of my father's money, let alone his personality and strength of will.

Once it was decided, I was all in. Our wedding was proof to me that I had been right all along, that love does conquer all, including racism, that the decisions I had made since junior year of high school had been justified. I didn't acknowledge how James might have felt sidelined by Daddy's role in James's own wedding, as if James didn't matter, and the two most important people in this wedding were me and Daddy. I didn't acknowledge it because I thought it was obvious that this was the right thing to do. I was an accidental rebel, not a real one. I never wanted to defy the rules or norms of our family or town. I didn't want to fight authority (what was right or acceptable), but what happened to me on July 26, 1969, changed everything about how this young girl felt about her parents, the community I grew up in, and the town I loved.

My rebellion didn't happen on purpose or all at once. Like most young people, I wanted to be liked and admired—and I was! In fact, I was popular and friendly to everyone. I saw myself as a nice girl, not a rebel. But being forced to come face-to-face with the racism in my community—and my family—had changed me. It woke me up big time. Then, over many decades, I became even more aware of how my gender and my Whiteness colored the way I looked at the world and the way the world looked at me. It took me years of therapy and self-reflection to understand and be able to talk about my experiences.

As soon as marrying James became a reality, the good girl in me wanted this marriage to make everything okay—okay with my family, okay with society, and most of all okay with me. It never occurred to me that James might have wanted something different. This was my privilege talking. James should have been honored to marry me, so now that I had decided and my father had given his blessing (or was it the other way around?), we were getting married, damn it.

Our marriage took place on July 29, 1978, the same date Princess Di and Prince Charles were married three years later. That date was also three days after the ninth anniversary of us getting caught together as teenagers and threatened with murder.

Our wedding wasn't huge. Daddy paid for everything as promised: my dress, the flowers, the guys' tuxes, and the reception, which took place on the top floor of a hotel in Santa Monica, overlooking the ocean. The wedding ceremony was in a small wedding chapel nearby. My dress was a lacy beige. I had no veil, but I had flowers in my hair that matched the bouquet I carried. Mary was my bridesmaid. Henry was James's best man. Claire stayed in Kentucky with Mom.

Recently I learned that James had picked Henry as his best man instead of his closer friend Willis because Henry was lighter-skinned and better educated than Willis. James thought Henry would be more acceptable to my father, which is ironic because, of all the people at the wedding, Daddy got along best with Willis, who was from Louisiana and had the same rough southern sense of humor my father had; he could drink with the best of them. Willis and Daddy matched each other drink for drink and cracked each other up all night long.

My sister Mary's husband William was there too, as was Daddy's second wife Nancy, and of course Henry's wife and my close friend Mary. To this day, Henry wonders about the brown tuxedoes all the men wore. They flattered nobody, Henry remembers, shaking his head. What was I thinking? What I was thinking was that the tuxes matched my beige dress, nothing more and nothing less.

The only regret I had about the wedding was that Mom chose not to attend, and because Mom wasn't there, Claire wasn't there either. Not only was Mom angry that I had been sneaking around with James all those years, but she also took it as a slap in the face that Nancy would be at the wedding. Nancy had been mean to Mom. Really mean. When Daddy and Nancy first got together before Mom and Dad had even separated, Nancy had tormented my mother with drunken late-night phone calls crowing about how Daddy loved her more than he loved Mom. Mom was not generally a weeper, but these calls sent her to her bedroom crying. Hearing that Nancy would be at the wedding must have been a huge flashback for Mom, a betrayal, a punch in the gut. I wish I could have pleased everybody, but that isn't always possible.

Mom didn't speak to me for eight months after I told her about James, but eventually we started talking again. Daddy, Mary, or Claire may have had something to do with that. All I know is I often tried to call Mom during that time, and either she wouldn't answer, or she'd make an excuse and quickly get off the phone. Then one day I called expecting the usual brush-off, and instead of making an excuse to hang up, Mom just started talking as if nothing had come between us.

James and I visited her and her new partner Rob a few times in Arizona after our reconciliation. Mom and Rob never married or even lived together, though I think Rob proposed to her often enough. She wanted nothing to do with a second marriage. Mom felt that Daddy had rescued her from Germany, and she never stopped loving him. She had a good time with Rob. They ate out, they went dancing, they invested in real estate together, but one marriage had been enough for her. Mom treated us well on these visits. She accepted that James was my husband, though I can't say she was ever completely comfortable with it.

Daddy had changed his mind about James as well. Daddy had this thing about family, like we were some kind of clan or tribe (and he was the chief, of course). Now that James had married me, James was family. James was in, as if a switch had been thrown.

Daddy still acted the big man with us, but he was friendly about it. One time James and I flew back to Kentucky and stayed with Daddy on the lake. He let James use his Cadillac to visit James's family, and James had an accident on the drive. Daddy was very gracious about it, though, telling James not to worry and taking care of the repairs himself. The local paper carried a short blurb: "James Jackson was involved in a minor accident on Hood Avenue on Tuesday. There were no injuries." The blurb ended by mentioning the car was registered to my father. A Black man driving a White man's Cadillac would have been unfathomable just ten years before. Daddy was always full of surprises, sometimes in a good way. In a strange twist, Daddy's third wife had a mixed-race child from a previous marriage, and he treated this child as his own.

All was not perfect in paradise, however. I ignored a huge red flag after the wedding. James got so drunk at the reception that we couldn't go on our honeymoon, a motel on Pacific Coast Highway in Malibu. I remember walking around our apartment in my wedding dress, spitting mad, him in his brown tuxedo passed out on the couch. I couldn't believe he had gotten so drunk we couldn't go on our honeymoon. Our friends had left us champagne and flowers in the hotel room, which we had to pick up the next day.

Once I was able to set the anger aside about the honeymoon, however, I felt as if a huge weight had been lifted from my shoulders now that we were married. Things would be different, I thought. I could truly reinvent myself.

Chapter 9

THE BEGINNING
OF THE END

But things weren't different. Life with James didn't get any easier just because we were married. In some ways, it got harder, or maybe I just started to notice the warning signs flashing everywhere.

The general vibe in Los Angeles was more accepting of interracial couples, and especially once we were married, I felt comfortable with us as a couple, both in public and private. Our friend Henry talks about Los Angeles as the first place he ever felt he belonged too, that he could be himself as a Black man. LA is a mix of many different cultures, and I loved that about the city—still do.

James never really believed that, though. He was never completely comfortable with us being together, in Los Angeles or anywhere else. He still didn't like to hold my hand or show any other signs of public affection, and that hurt. I shouldn't have expected him to change overnight, I guess, but I was hoping. I saw this as a continuation of the secrecy we moved to LA and got married to avoid.

Here's an example. The guys—Willis, Henry, and James—were on a basketball team in a park league, and sometimes Mary and I would watch them play. I love sports. I love to cheer for sports. I can be pretty loud about it when my man is playing. I didn't get up and do my old cheer routines. I just clapped and hollered when anybody did something good, and sometimes I got the crowd going with me. But James didn't like that. He wanted me to be quieter, more sedate, to not call attention to myself. He didn't like it that I was so outgoing. He didn't like it that I had a lot of friends. He wanted me to be seen and not heard.

And sometimes not even seen.

Willis, who was single, liked to throw parties, but whenever one came up, James would tell me, "It's just the guys. The guys are getting together."

I'd say, "Okay." I had no problem with guys' nights. But then I'd find out later there were plenty of women at the party, and I wondered why James didn't want me to go. I had my suspicions, but it wasn't until years later that Henry and Willis confirmed that James saw these parties as hunting grounds, so he could meet women and sleep around. Henry and Willis said they hated the way he treated me like that, that James was, in their words, a "skank" about it. If James knew a woman had been with another guy, he saw her as fair game and would do things like go to that woman's house and knock on the door to see if she'd sleep with him too. (You know, because once you sleep with one guy, you should sleep with them all!) He had no respect for boundaries, no character. If he met a woman who caught his attention, even if she was with someone else—even if she was with one of his friends—he'd slip his business card into her pocket or handbag. But Willis and Henry felt they couldn't say anything, either to him or to me.

At the same time, James refused to go with me to any of my work events. As a sales rep firm, we had many events with clients. James resented me going without him, but he didn't want to go with me either. A catch-22. I couldn't say no to the events, though—that was my job! Besides, I love parties. He claimed it wasn't easy for him to talk to people he didn't know, but come on, he worked at an insurance company where he had to talk to strangers. I think he didn't feel comfortable going to *my* work events—with *me*. Most of the people at these events were White, and James didn't like to stand out. He felt exposed, out of his element, or so he claimed. He worked with White people all day long, and that didn't seem to bother him. It just seemed to me that he didn't want to hang out with *my* White people. Maybe these events were boring for him, or he truly wasn't comfortable spending time with all those White people in his leisure hours. He should have let me go alone with his blessing, not pout or get angry about it.

If James didn't have something of his own to do on the nights I had an event, he'd sit at home drinking and stewing, watching the clock like a prison warden, counting the seconds until my return. He acted as if he owned me. He criticized me in front of other people so often that I became self-conscious. I had to watch what I did. It was that same kind of walking on eggshells with our father we had to do when I was a kid. If I was going to be later than I told him, I had to call, or I'd get yelled at when I got home. Sometimes James would be furious with me even when I did call or came home on time, especially if I was in a good mood, like I had had too much of a good time. If I had to go out without him for work, in James's mind, I could at least have the good grace to have a bad time. He'd be drunk and spouting all kinds of nonsense about me checking out other guys and stepping out on him, which I now know is a classic tactic of cheaters everywhere: accusing their romantic partners of doing exactly what they're doing.

When he got mad, he'd first yell, but then he'd give me that silent treatment for days. He absolutely would not talk to me, which drove me nuts. If you haven't figured it out by now, I'm a talker. If you've got something to say, let's have it out. But that was the problem. He didn't have something to say; he just wanted to punish me. I'd be in the kitchen slamming cabinet doors, trying to get a rise out of him, his silence building up the pressure in me until I was ready to explode. I was living with this man, my husband, presumably the love of my life, and he would not talk to me. I know now this is another form of control and emotional abuse. Back then I just thought he was being a jerk. And since I had grown up with my father, I was used to this kind of behavior. That's how I thought men were. They didn't allow themselves to feel anything but anger, which they numbed by drinking or let out in a rage.

I realize now that I was codependent with the two most important men in my life: my father and my husband. I tolerated the drinking and the rage and made excuses for them. Sure, their behavior made me angry. I'd yell at them in my head and sometimes even out loud, but I never tried to set any boundaries. I never tried to talk to either of them in a healthy, adult-to-adult way. Not that either of them would have been open to that kind of discussion, but still, I never really tried. That's on me.

I didn't really do anything about it, until one night . . .

. . . James hit me.

He was drunk, as was par for the course at this point in our marriage, and we were probably arguing about something stupid, as we did just about every night by then. Maybe I had come in later than I had said I would. I don't remember. I had had a couple of drinks myself, and I was tired of getting the third degree every time I walked into the apartment. He seemed particularly enraged that night, but I didn't back down, and something I said—maybe I told him to cut it out and leave me alone, or maybe I called him an asshole—flipped the switch, and he swung at me, punched me in the eye.

We both froze, stunned. He had never hit me before. No man except my father had ever hit me. His face collapsed into shame, guilt, fear, anger, and concern all at once. I was scared. All I could think about was the gun under the bed my father had given me for the trip to California. He seemed angry enough to use it. I ran into the bathroom, shut the door, and locked it. My eye was watering and puffing shut already. I was going to have serious bruises, and all of a sudden, I knew that after twelve years together and two years of marriage, I was done. It was as if my own switch had finally clicked off. I was saying to myself, *No. This is it. No. No, no man's ever going to touch me like that again. Not ever again. This is it.* Because even after all Daddy did to Mom, he never hit her. That was the line. Daddy never hit Mom, so when James hit me, that was it. James and I were done.

I didn't leave that night, but it was over. Emotionally I was done. James had a nasty side that came out when he was drinking, and by the end of our marriage, he was drinking morning until night.

I couldn't go to work the next day. A friend called, and I told her what happened. "Are you okay? Can I bring you something?" She didn't wait for an answer; she came over right away. When she saw my eye, which was black and blue and almost swollen shut, she said, "That asshole. Look what he's done to you."

I told James we were finished. He wouldn't leave the apartment, so I had to. This was early 1980. We had been married for only two years.

James was devastated when I left. He didn't understand. Believe it or not, he truly didn't understand why I would want to leave him, even after he punched me in the eye. "How can you do this to me?" he said over and over during one of our arguments. "How can you do this to me?"

"How can you do *this* to me?" I said, pointing to my eye, though he couldn't see it through the door. At this point all our conversations had a door between us.

"That's nothing," he said. "That's one time."

"That's all it takes," I said.

"I'll never do it again. One time, that's nothing."

"I know you won't because we are done!"

Once it sunk in that I was really leaving, James stopped going to work. His friends said they couldn't get him out of bed. He drank all day and played Willie Nelson's "Always on My Mind" over and over and over on the stereo, driving his friends a little crazy.

I guess I should have been flattered by his reaction, but by then James had worn me down, destroying any of the love we might have once had for each other. It's not like he couldn't have seen the split coming, what with all his cheating and fighting, but I think he was truly shocked. He had always gotten his way. I had never really stood up to him before. Maybe he thought I was bluffing.

I left a day or two later and stayed with a friend in Hollywood Hills for three or four days. James had pulled himself out of bed and begged me to come back. He went as far as agreeing to couples counseling, which I had been trying to get us to do for months. We had two sessions with a therapist on Mulholland Drive, but it was too late. It wasn't going to work. I didn't love him anymore.

Meanwhile, I returned to the apartment and stayed for a few weeks, the whole time secretly putting things in place to move out and finalize the divorce. At this point, I was afraid of James, of what he was capable of doing. He was a big, angry man. Each day, I waited until he left for work to do anything about the move so I wouldn't rile him. We didn't talk much—he was giving me the silent treatment—but when we did talk, I always spoke very calmly, diplomatically, to ease the tension and to keep from setting him off.

At night I fell asleep on the couch once he drank his fill, turned off the TV, and stumbled into bed.

When I left for good and got my own place, I let James have just about everything. We had a furnished apartment, so we didn't have much to divide, just kitchen stuff like pots and pans, bathroom towels, sheets and blankets, the usual stuff a household collects over the years. I went there with my friend Edie to pick up my share, and James was drunk and ugly since I was sticking to my decision to leave. He really believed he could charm me into staying, and when he realized that wasn't going to happen, he stood in the living room and yelled at us, "Hurry up. Get your shit and get the fuck out of here." He scared us, and we threw things into boxes haphazardly. Finally James said, "That's it. You don't get anything else. Get the fuck out of here." So we did. We practically ran out of that apartment with my few boxes. James is a large man. It wasn't worth the risk for a few pots and pans.

I had found an apartment on Venice Boulevard, where I slept on a mattress on the floor for the first month. My mother happily flew in from Arizona to help me shop for furniture and set up the new place. Mom never said so directly, but I think she was thrilled that James and I had split for good, both for my safety—I had told her about some of James's increasingly abusive behavior—and because she no longer had to explain a Black son-in-law. Once James and I were married, Mom had reluctantly accepted that we were in a "mixed marriage," as she would have called it, but deep down I don't think she ever approved.

The divorce came through in January 1981, and I was relieved and sad at the same time. I was relieved because now I'd be able to put this whole sordid mess behind me and truly reinvent myself. I was sad because I had invested nearly half my life until then fighting for something I thought was real but turned out to be a mirage—our love for each other. In some ways, James and I were like many couples that split up. We had some good times, and we had some very bad times. However, on top of that, we also battled significant cultural challenges. We faced racism and abortions and infidelity together, but we never really learned to talk to each other, to understand each other, to figure each other out. We probably shouldn't have been a couple. We probably wouldn't have been a couple for as long as we were if we had simply been allowed to date in high school. The relationship likely would have run the natural course of many high school relationships, fading once the initial excitement cooled and we realized we didn't have much in com-mon. We stayed together longer than we should have because so many people told us we shouldn't, and neither of us liked to be told what to do. We stayed together out of pure cussedness, and that did neither of us any good.

Chapter 10

MY NEW LIFE

My experience with James has been central to my life, but I have lived another full life since then.

I was single for about five years after the divorce—from age twenty-nine to thirty-four. During that time, I thrived. I made good money as a sales rep and moved into a more upscale apartment. Divorced from James, and with Daddy back in Kentucky and Mom in Arizona, I had no one to answer to for the first time in my life. I decorated my apartment the way I wanted to, kept my own schedule, ate cereal for dinner when I felt like it. I dated during this time, but nothing very serious. I played the field. I enjoyed my independence.

After about five years single, I met David through my sister Claire. They were both in the film business and worked at the same visual effects company. The team often went out for drinks after work, and one night Claire said, "Why don't you join us?" and I did.

I dated a friend of David's for a while, but David was always saying things to him like, "I don't know why you don't marry this girl. This is the greatest girl. She's one in a million. If you don't marry her, someone else is going to snatch her up." And then one night David and I got into an intense conversation, and the sparks flew. David impressed me with his intelligence and passion for his career. He was also White and genuinely a nice man. I had had enough trauma married to a Black man who took his anger out on me. I was ready for something different, and yes, that was part of the attraction. But it's not like I jumped into a serious relationship with the first White guy I met after the divorce. This was five years later. I had dated men of different races in that time. David was the first one I wanted to spend the rest of my life with.

David and I dated for a year, then married. I was thirty-five, David a year older.

But I never do anything the easy way. David had a daughter from his first marriage; I didn't have any children of my own. I wanted to have a baby with David, and David wanted to have a baby with me, and my biological clock was ticking. Although I continued to work after we married, I was in my midthirties, so we started trying for a baby right away.

Here's where the universe can kick you in the teeth. I didn't have trouble getting pregnant in my thirties, but now I couldn't carry a pregnancy to term. I had a series of devastating miscarriages. We thought maybe work was too stressful, so I stopped working at age thirty-eight, but the miscarriages continued, each one more heart-breaking than the last.

I had eight miscarriages before we found a doctor who helped couples experiencing multiple miscarriages. He and his colleagues studied how the body's immune response can affect pregnancy and cause miscarriage. In simple terms, my body treated the pregnancy as an invader and attacked the fetus as if it were a disease. This had something to do with how my genetic material mixed with David's—together we created too many antigens or something like that, which caused my body to overreact and essentially kill the fetus.

The solution—again in very simple terms—was to spin David's white blood cells, treat them somehow so they wouldn't be as deadly to the fetus, and transfuse them into me. Because the doctor's approach was so revolutionary, we did one of the procedures on *The Today Show* with Katie Couric! The procedure did the trick. When I got pregnant this time, my body was no longer programmed to kill the fetus, and our son Daniel was born in 1992 when I was forty.

Friends (and my therapist) have asked me whether I was ever afraid the abortions earlier in my life were somehow related to the miscarriages. If they meant were the miscarriages some kind of divine retribution, then absolutely not. I gave up all belief in God when the church turned on me in high school. If they meant physically, I still say no, especially after the doctor explained that the likely cause of the miscarriages was a mismatch of my genes and David's. Besides, I had put that all behind me. I was so focused on the present and the future that I didn't have time to dwell on the past.

⑤ ⑤ ⑤

It wasn't easy being an older mom. Taking care of a baby was very physical, and I was tired a lot of the time. But I wouldn't trade it for anything.

David was in the film business in visual effects with Disney for eight years as a department head. Then he established and ran his own shop for the next seventeen years. The work was all-engrossing and virtually 24/7. He worked very hard until about ten years ago, when he suffered an aneurysm and had open heart surgery to replace an aortic valve. After that, he was forced to retire. The film business is nothing if not stressful.

Having David home full time was an adjustment, but we've arrived at the point in our lives where we are both content with ourselves and each other, where we appreciate each other's good qualities and tolerate the quirks, and that helps immensely.

Daniel has grown into a fine young man, and that's not just a proud mom talking. He's smart and caring and wants to bring about social justice in the world in ways big and small. He decided on this path after we took a family trip to Bali when he was in high school. He was struck by the contrast between his life in a ritzy private school in Southern California and the poverty we encountered in Bali, how the poor lived in shacks without plumbing or electricity. He vowed to return to the United States to get the education he needed to help him do something about it.

And that's what he did. Daniel finished high school, then earned a degree in international studies at the University of Oregon. He moved to Argentina and later to Nicaragua to work with NGOs. He's been in Mexico the last five years, where he started an organization for students doing international nonprofit work to learn and practice languages. He came back to Los Angeles for a two-year master's program at University of California, Los Angeles. We loved spending time with him face-to-face, along with David's daughter and her husband, who also live in Los Angeles. It was good to have our family in one place for a change.

Once Daniel finished the program at UCLA, he moved back to Oaxaca, Mexico, to help the Indigenous populations with smart agricultural methods and micro-financing. He recently learned how to build a composting toilet. We miss him dearly.

Daniel also attributes his search for justice and the career he's chosen to my time with James. I never held back anything about my story from Daniel. He grew angry for me about the injustices James and I faced. He was one of the first to encourage me to write this book.

Chapter 11

FINAL REFLECTIONS

I recently celebrated my seventy-second birthday, and that's one of the reasons I want to tell my story: to look back so I can look forward. David and I have a lot of life left to live, and I want to release some things from my past so I can live free from the baggage.

People I've told this story to have been encouraging me to write a book for many years, but it's only recently I've felt the strength and perspective to do so. Now that I'm older and not caught up in the immediate drama and trauma of the story, I can feel it and experience it in a different way, see it as an important part of my life that brought me to where I am.

I think my story is an important slice of American history, as well as a painful but ultimately rewarding life journey. For a long time I thought no one would believe me, that things had changed enough in the world regarding race that my story would seem like ancient history. Now I'm not so sure. The hatred unleashed in the 2016, 2020, and 2024 election cycles suggests otherwise.

I wish the story of me and James could have been the happily-ever-after of fairy tales, but it wasn't. I stuck with James for so long and eventually married him to prove that my parents and the rest of the town were wrong. I don't think James ever really wanted to get married. We lived in the South. He was the Black star basketball player dating a White star cheerleader. As teenagers, we were sneaking around; it was dangerous for both of us. As adults, we kept sneaking around until we moved to Los Angeles where we eventually married.

James's friends point out that James had always been hyper-concerned about what people thought of him, that he always worried about doing the wrong thing. That concern was magnified when James was with me since he had to negotiate the White world with a White girlfriend, then a White wife. James wouldn't eat certain foods in the presence of White people—watermelon, rice, and fried chicken in particular—because he knew White society often considered it the stereotypical foods of Black people. He didn't want to call attention to his Blackness. Maybe he felt that my father (and me?) had forced him into a marriage he didn't really want, and he expressed his anger and resentment by drinking, cheating on, and abusing me.

He was controlling and abusive. I was a naive, sometimes clueless White woman, and later in our relationship, I think he also saw me as a source of financial stability. Sure, James always had a job, but whenever we did anything big, it was usually my money (or my father's) that paid for it: going out to clubs, renting apartments, moving to Los Angeles, the wedding, and the divorce. Ultimately, James and I had a love-hate relationship. He called me ugly. He didn't want me to put myself out there, to succeed at what I did, perhaps out of fear that he'd lose me and because he wanted to keep me all to himself. And because he didn't want me to outshine him. It was the age-old story of any dysfunctional, abusive relationship with the racial component added to make it all the more complex, confusing, and painful.

Once we married, we soon discovered there was nothing there. James turned out to be a mean alcoholic like my father, and just as my father had cheated on my mother, James cheated on me—early and often. James tried to excuse it once by saying all the men he knew slept around. It didn't mean anything. It was just sex.

Yeah, I don't buy that, not anymore. James was somewhat religious, always talking about "God providing" this or that, but what about "thou shalt forsake all others" once you're married? At some point, cheating becomes a choice, and he chose to cheat on me. And like many cheaters, he was convinced I was cheating on him at the same time, so he became deeply jealous and controlling. At one point, I had to account for every second of my time—where I went, who I was with, what we did, how long we were there. It was exhausting. He wanted me to stay home and wait for him on the couch, the demure, dutiful wife, while he was out doing whatever he wanted, drinking and carousing and sleeping with any woman who would have him. He married the wrong girl if he thought that was ever going to happen.

He was shocked and devastated when we split up, but I was done. He never understood what broke the marriage. To him, the cheating was recreational, like the pickup basketball he played with his friends. And the controlling jealousy? That just showed how much he loved me, how much he cared. We never really talked about the punch to the face. For a while I looked the other way about the cheating—and the jealousy and the control and the emotional abuse—because I am a stubborn woman, and no one was going to tell me I had made a bad choice. James bears much of the responsibility for what he put me through, for treating me the way he did. But I bear my share as well, especially as the codependent daughter of an alcoholic. If I hadn't been so damn stubborn, I could have freed us both to live our own lives much sooner. I ignored the signs that James was not a good partner because I was desperately seeking vindication, and the only way I was going to get it was by soldiering on and making it to marriage no matter what.

We made it to marriage all right, after nine years of banging our heads against the brick wall of racism. This despite the fact that neither of us thought of ourselves as crusaders. This wasn't really political for us; it was personal, and on some level, we didn't feel that we had a choice. You can argue, no, you always have a choice. But we—let's say *I*, since I can't speak for James—didn't feel that we had a choice. That to justify our being together and all the trauma that came with that, the emotional abuse we both experienced, the physical abuse I experienced, we had to get married. This is likely how my father saw it too, as his way of vindicating his own over-the-top racist reactions THAT DAY. *See, they got married. It all worked out.*

I know there's a fine line between explanation and justification that I'm likely stomping all over here. I know that I'm not the saint in all this, that I'm not the only victim. Given the years since then, I wonder now if James ever felt he had a real choice about any of it. In many ways I am my father's daughter, and once I get on a train, I ride it to the end. At the time, I thought it was the natural best step—Daddy says it's time to get married, so it's time to get married. I'm not sure I ever asked James what he thought, deep down, about what we should do, or listened to his answer if I did. Only now do I see that James had become something like a game piece in my lifelong battle to both please my father and rebel against him. For this I am sorry.

When James and I actually got married, we found it was a place neither of us really wanted to be. Whatever had made us fall in love had been ground down and flushed away by all we had been through.

I've come to understand this is not unusual for interracial couples. According to a Pew Research Center study analyzing data from the 1990s, after ten years of marriage, interracial couples had a 41 percent chance of separation or divorce, while couples of the same race had a 31 percent chance.[6] What mix of races within the couples had the highest chance of divorce or separation? A Black husband and a White wife. The odds were against us from the start. What relationship could carry the weight of such expectations during that time?

In the end, when I think about whether it was all worth it, I come to this: The suffering was greater than the joy. I often wonder what my life would have been like if I had not been with James and experienced the trauma this relationship caused. Would my life have been easier? Would I have been healthier emotionally? I hesitate to say I regret this part of my life, and I can't exactly say I wish I hadn't been with James, but I do wonder. Part of me will always wonder, and I will never really know. Because I *was* with James, and this is the life I've led.

---

[6]"The Rise of Intermarriage: Rates, Characteristics Vary by Race and Gender," Pew Research Center, February 16, 2012, https://www.pewresearch.org/social-trends/2012/02/16/chapter-1-overview/.

EPILOGUE

In 2010, I went home for my high school class's fortieth reunion. It wasn't *my* fortieth reunion since I had graduated from the boarding school. I was reluctant to go, but my therapist encouraged me to attend to face my demons and get some closure.

It took a lot of nerve for me to go back, but I'm glad I did. I met up with Grace, and we attended all the events together. I was able to spend time with her and Bobby, both of whom always "got" me, always had empathy for what I had experienced dating James. It was a relief to be able to talk with complete openness about it, to feel heard. Once I married James, my family accepted the idea of him and me together (however reluctantly), but they never really wanted to talk about what had come before our marriage in any great detail. In their minds, getting married to James meant that everything had worked out just fine, so why bring up all that bad history? Grace and Bobby didn't shove my experience under the rug, and that was a relief.

At the reunion, I felt as if I was on stage the whole time. People wanted to see what had become of me, some for a voyeuristic thrill, I'm sure, but others out of genuine concern. I had been well-liked at school, at the center of our social world. When the organizers of the reunion invited me to attend, I responded to their email with something like, "You know I didn't graduate from the high school, right?"

They were very sweet in their response. "Maybe not, but you'll always be part of our class."

Most of those attending the reunion hadn't seen me since I was sixteen. Even to this day, when people from town see me or hear my name or the family name, that's the first thing they remember: the Scandal. Because that's how the town saw it—as a big, juicy, entertaining Scandal, with a capital *S*. So I was surprised when one female classmate came up to me and said, "You know, that was awful what happened to you. It was terrible the way you were treated." And I believe she meant it. I hadn't expected much sympathy from anyone really. Many others over the weekend said similar things. I responded to them all with some version of, "Thank you for saying that. I'm still in therapy to recover." At the same time, I was moved and grateful for their genuine good wishes.

Grace observed that people were genuinely happy to see me, that many people had been fond of me, and they were glad to see that I had come out all right. Her theory is that in many ways, James and I, because of who we were—a star basketball player and a prominent cheerleader—we were game changers for the town. According to Grace, we cracked things open a bit for other mixed-race couples, and we educated members of the town.

Maybe. I hope so. I'd like to think that's what happened, even if only to a small degree, that what we went through—what many of their own families had put us through, let's be honest—made people stop and think that maybe the hate and racism didn't have to go on forever.

I'd like to be remembered for something other than the Scandal, but that's the path my life has taken. It made me who I am today, for good and bad, and I've been trying to deal with it for a long time. Maybe I would have been happier if none of it had happened. Maybe I wouldn't have ended up with an alcoholic and emotionally abusive partner if my relationship with my father had been different. Having worked with a therapist for sixteen years, I'm stronger and healthier now.

My parents never really talked with me about THAT DAY. Like many families, we preferred not to think about the bad stuff. The worse it was, the less we talked about it. And what could be worse than trying to kill your own daughter for dating a Black man? For the rest of my parents' lives, we treated the events of July 26, 1969—and the whole time I had spent with James before we got married—as if none of it had ever happened. Maybe if we had talked about it, I wouldn't have been so gung ho to stay with James to prove that I was right and they were wrong.

I take that back. Daddy did talk about it once, when I was visiting him at the Mansion, as we called it, his home in Kentucky. He was sitting in his chair in the bedroom holding forth like he did. This was after James and I had divorced but before I married David, so more than thirty-five years ago. Daddy told me, "You know what happened a long time ago?" I knew exactly what he meant, the night he found James and me together. "It wasn't right. It shouldn't have happened like that."

That was it. That was all he ever said, and that's as close as he came to an apology.

I forgave Daddy, and we became very close over the years, believe it or not. In some stretches we talked on the phone almost every day. He was a lot of fun. He was a real character, and he loved sports. We had a lot in common. All of us sisters forgave him. It was the right thing to do.

Many of my friends, as well as David and even my therapist, wonder how I can forgive Daddy with the way he treated me, how I could have stayed so close to him. My therapist puts it this way: "Why do you always take up for him?"

And what I say in response is, "He was my father." That's how I was raised. If my mother could forgive him for what he did to her, I could certainly forgive him for what he did to me.

And what good would come from holding a grudge? I forgave Daddy long ago—and Mom too. Once we began speaking again after James and I got married, I talked to her on the phone every day, sometimes more than once. In their own way, albeit a way that was infected by the bigotry, racism, and misogyny they grew up with, they did what they did in part to protect me, misguided as that may have been. Until the day they died (Dad in 2007 and Mom in 2018), they did what they did from a place of love, a love laced with fear, yes, and a love they expressed in ways that were not always healthy, but love, nonetheless. To move on with my life without bitterness—to get the most out of the time I have left—that's what I choose to remember.

ACKNOWLEDGMENTS

I'd like to thank all my friends and family who have supported me by listening to my story over the years and helping me process the experience.

I'd like to especially thank Grace, Bobby, and Henry, not only for their friendship and support but also for agreeing to be interviewed for this book.

I'd also like to thank my therapist of about sixteen years for encouraging me to tell my story, first in our sessions, then for the wider world.

I thank my sisters for all their support throughout the years, as well as my parents, with whom I forged a loving relationship despite what happened THAT DAY, July 26, 1969.

I'd also like to thank Charles Grosel of Write for Success for helping me bring my story to the page and putting this book together, as well as Laura Bush, PhD, of Peacock Proud Press for bringing it to print.

ABOUT THE AUTHOR

B orn and raised in Kentucky during the 1950s and 60s, Annie Waxman, a pen name, witnessed firsthand the impacts of systemic racism and cultural resistance to change. Her memoir, *Accidental Rebel: My Story of Interracial Love and Loss*, offers a deeply personal perspective on love, racial identity, and life in the segregated South. Now living in California, Annie reflects on her journey with insight and wisdom. She writes to help readers understand the past, foster growth, and live free of prejudice and abuse.